YEARBOOK 2010/11

Supported by
ARTS COUNCIL ENGLAND

First published in 2010 by the Royal Opera House
in association with Oberon Books Ltd

Oberon Books
521 Caledonian Road, London N7 9RH
Tel 020 7607 3637 Fax 020 7607 3629
info@oberonbooks.com
www.oberonbooks.com

Original cover and book design: Jeff Willis

Cover and book design 2010: James Illman

Royal Opera House Project Manager: Will Richmond

Editor: Andrew Walby

Royal Opera House Commissioning Editor: John Snelson

Every effort has been made to trace the copyright holders of all images reprinted in this book. Acknowledgement is made in all cases where the image source is available, but we would be grateful for information about any images where sources could not be traced.

A catalogue record for this book is available from the British Library.

ISBN 987-1-84943-002-9

Printed and bound in Great Britain by CPI Antony Rowe, Chippenham.

Royal Opera House
Covent Garden
London WC2E 9DD
Box Office 020 7304 4000
www.roh.org.uk

*Front cover: Marianela Nuñez as Sphinx
and Rupert Pennefather as Oedipus in Glen Tetley's* Sphinx.
Photograph: Bill Cooper
Back cover: The Royal Ballet in Kenneth MacMillan's Elite
Syncopations
Photograph: Johan Persson
*Inside front cover and title page: Dancers of The Royal Ballet in
Liam Scarlett's* Asphodel Meadows.
Photograph: Johan Persson
*Inside back cover: Dancers of The Royal Ballet rehearse Jonathan
Watkins's* As One
Photograph: Bill Cooper
Photograph of Monica Mason on page 4 by Johan Persson

Contents

Welcome from Monica Mason

It's not difficult to pick out the highlights of the 2009/10 Season, although there is much to look back on that was very rewarding – individual performances, debuts, and some great moments from the corps de ballet. But I am especially proud that two of the three new ballets presented on the main stage were by young choreographers who are members of the Company, Liam Scarlett and Jonathan Watkins.

In addition to creating his own works for us, Resident Choreographer Wayne McGregor is instrumental in encouraging the next generation of choreographic talent from within both the Company and The Royal Ballet School. This was nowhere more evident than in the performances of New Works in the Linbury last June which were choreographed entirely by Company members and made a hugely entertaining programme.

The 2010/11 Season also promises to be an exciting one. Christopher Wheeldon will create his first full-length work for the Company, *Alice's Adventures in Wonderland*, to receive its premiere in February 2011. There will be more new work from Kim Brandstrup and Wayne McGregor as well as major revivals of several ballets not seen for some time.

I hope very much that you will enjoy this latest edition of our Yearbook and also the many varied programmes to come in the Season ahead.

Monica Mason

Dame Monica Mason DBE
Director, The Royal Ballet

The Company

The Royal Ballet Tour, Summer 2009

After a very busy end to the 2008/9 Season, The Royal Ballet left London immediately for Washington D.C. for a tour that took in the American capital, the gorgeous gardens of the Alhambra in Granada, Spain, and the tropical heat of Havana, Cuba – home of Royal Ballet Principal Guest Artist Carlos Acosta. First, the Company took over the stage at the Kennedy Center for six nights and a matinee, giving five performances of *Manon* and two performances of a mixed programme that featured McGregor's *Chroma*, Wheeldon's *DGV: Danse à grande vitesse* and Ashton's *A Month in the Country*. From Washington they went to Granada and performed *Swan Lake* twice at the Generalife Gardens before flying to Cuba.

At the Gran Teatro in Havana the three performances of a mixed programme again included *Chroma* and *A Month in the Country*, but added a selection of *pas de deux* including *Voices of Spring*, *Romeo and Juliet* (balcony scene), *Winter Dreams* (Farewell), *Thaïs*, *Le Corsaire*, *Theme and Variations*, *Swan Lake Act III*, *Don Quixote* and *Giselle Act II*. It also included *Les Lutins*, the *pas de trois* choreographed by Johan Kobborg for New Works in the Linbury earlier in the Season, and a change of cast for this resulted in the opportunity of an unscheduled debut for Artist James Hay. The Royal Ballet's visit was a major event in Cuba, and the extraordinarily enthusiastic reception of the Company's performers and performances (along with some of the technical complications!) were captured in a television documentary by Michael Nunn and William Trevitt (the Balletboyz) broadcast over Christmas.

The Opening of the Season

After a much needed break the 2009/10 Season opened with high drama: Kenneth MacMillan's *Mayerling*, his intense psychological interpretation of the violent events surrounding the double suicide of Crown Prince Rudolf of Austria Hungary and his mistress Mary Vetsera. The first night was a special performance supported by the Helen Hamlyn Trust and, in association with *The Sun* newspaper, gave a chance for audiences completely new to ballet to discover both the art and pleasure of the splendid Royal Opera House. Not surprisingly, it was a full house. During the run of *Mayerling*, no less than five of the Company's Principal men took on the role of Rudolf – possibly one of the most challenging ever created for a male dancer – with impressive debuts from Rupert Pennefather and Thiago Soares; three Principal women played Mary Vetsera during the run, as well as First Artist Melissa Hamilton (now a Soloist) in a well-received role debut.

Embracing the Royal Opera House's explosion of multimedia, a performance of *Mayerling* with Edward Watson, Mara Galeazzi and Sarah Lamb was recorded by Opus Arte, screened in cinemas worldwide and released on DVD and Blu-ray early in 2010. Likewise, 2010 saw the release of *Ondine* with Miyako Yoshida (also with Watson), *The Nutcracker* with Yoshida and McRae dancing the Grand *pas de deux*, and three MacMillan ballets from the mixed programme later in the Season (*Concerto*, *The Judas Tree* and *Elite Syncopations*).

Taking the Spotlight

In autumn, at the start of the Season, First Soloist Sergei Polunin was the featured artist for the 'World Stage' promotional material for the Royal Opera House – photographed in a striking setting in his native Ukraine. By the end of the Season, he had been promoted to Principal, and at the age of only 20 is one of the youngest dancers ever to reach the Company's highest rank. Through 2009/10, Polunin made four role debuts, including Prince Florimund in *The Sleeping Beauty* dancing with Hikaru Kobayashi as Princess Aurora. To great acclaim he also danced the Prince in *The Nutcracker*, with Sarah Lamb as his Sugar Plum Fairy. It was Lamb who took Polunin's position as the face of the Opera House for the Spring, photographed on pointe in the Grand Canyon, in her native Arizona, tying into her own role debut as Cinderella. Images and interviews about creating these dramatic photographs were featured on www.roh.org.uk, along with information about all performances and activities at the Royal Opera House through the year.

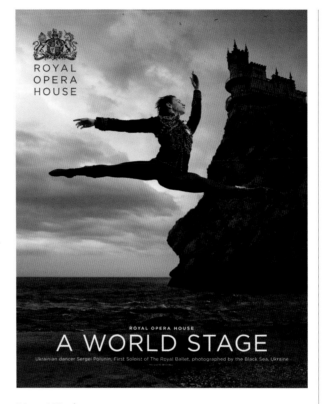

ROYAL OPERA HOUSE

A WORLD STAGE

Ukrainian dancer Sergei Polunin, First Soloist of The Royal Ballet, photographed by the Black Sea, Ukraine

New Works

With three world premieres, new choreographers on the main stage and the return of very recently created ballets, it has been a particularly creative Season for new work with The Royal Ballet. The first world premiere was in November, with *Limen*, an exciting new ballet from Resident Choreographer Wayne McGregor with music by Finnish composer Kaija Saariaho (in its British premiere) and designs by Japanese artist Tatsuo Miyajima. It was included in a mixed programme with Balanchine's *Agon* and, entering the Company's repertory for the first time, Glen Tetley's enigmatic *Sphinx*. Miyajima's designs included

7

his trademark LED counting numbers, projected onto a gauze drop, but as part of the designer's own philosophy on the inclusiveness of the creative process, everyone who had had any input – whether dancers or stage crew, costume makers or office staff – was invited to select a number position in the design, a number from which the counting would begin and a period of time that determined how quickly the number would change.

In February there were two first revivals of very recent new works in the same programme as another world premiere. Brandstrup's intense and evocative 2008 ballet *Rushes: Fragments of a Lost Story* and McGregor's 2009 smash hit *Infra*. The original cast returned with the exception of First Artist Jonathan Watkins whose *As One* was the first ballet of the mixed programme. This was an eagerly anticipated new ballet, not just for Watkins's distinctive and developing choreography and the commissioned score by Graham Fitkin, but also as his first work on the main stage.

Towards the end of the Season, the Company performed Wheeldon's *Electric Counterpoint* from 2008. *Counterpoint* appeared in a programme with Mats Ek's *Carmen* and Pompea Santoro returned to the House to stage the ballet. Completing this programme was another much anticipated world premiere. Royal Ballet First Artist Liam Scarlett choreographed his first piece for the Company on the main stage, *Asphodel Meadows*, and it was received with great admiration.

In the Linbury Studio Theatre, Kim Brandstrup had been invited by ROH2 right at the start of the Opera House Season to create a piece. In collaboration with Royal Ballet Principal Tamara Rojo, he created *Goldberg*, danced to J.S. Bach's *Goldberg Variations*, and invited Principal Steven McRae and Soloist Thomas Whitehead to dance as guests. *Goldberg* went on to win an Olivier award for Best New Dance Production. The revival of Brandstrup's *Rushes* on the main stage in February, brought back the original cast – Cojocaru, Morera, Acosta – but also brought Rojo back together with Whitehead and Leanne Benjamin. Brandstrup will be back early in the 2010/11 Season to create another new ballet for the Company for the main stage.

The annual New Works performances from The Royal Ballet in the Linbury Studio Theatre in June were sold out and enthusiastically received. Each year has yielded short new pieces by choreographic talent from within the Company, and this year had works by Viacheslav Samodurov, Ludovic Ondiviela, Vanessa Fenton, Alastair Marriott, Kristen McNally and Erico Montes. As in previous years, the styles and approaches were as eclectic as the choices of music (from Shostakovich to John Adams). Robert Clark and Kate Shipway provided superb musical accompaniment on pianos with Peter Adams on cello for two of the pieces and baritone Grant Doyle singing for

Alastair Marriott's *Lieder*. The whole occasion reflected The Royal Ballet's ongoing encouragement of new choreography from within its own ranks.

Royal Ballet Classics

Ashton's *Tales of Beatrix Potter* and *Les Patineurs* played to delighted audiences through Christmas and into the New Year. *La Fille mal gardée* – Ashton's bucolic idyll – received outstanding reviews from the critics, celebrating its 50th year as a much-loved landmark in the Company repertory. Guest Principal Miyako Yoshida took her final bow on the main stage as a Principal with the Company in the title role of *Cinderella*, another Ashton classic. Wayne Sleep returned to dance one of her Step-Sisters, alongside former Soloist Luke Heydon.

January 2010 brought the beginning of a run of performances of MacMillan's *Romeo and Juliet*, always an audience favourite. In celebration of MacMillan's unique talent and versatility – vital to shaping The Royal Ballet's style and repertory since the 1950s – in what would have been his 80th year the Company also presented three of his shorter ballets in a single programme that brought out the extraordinary range of the choreographer across forms, styles and themes: *Concerto*, *The Judas Tree* and *Elite Syncopations*. Jette Parker Young Artist Dominic Grier made his debut as a conductor for The Royal Ballet conducting *Concerto*, and Robert Clark, who takes over as Head of Music Staff in the new Season, conducted *Elite Syncopations* from the piano.

The Season Ends

The Season closed with another mixed programme: Wheeldon appearing again with his *Tryst* from 2002. Wheeldon returns in 2010/11 for a particularly exciting project – his creation of a new full-length ballet based on the story of *Alice's Adventures in Wonderland*.

Tryst was performed with McGregor's 2006 *Chroma* and Balanchine's *Symphony in C* – the last conducted again by Dominic Grier, and *Tryst* by James MacMillan, who also composed the music. This final programme was broadcast live as part of the BP Summer Big Screens, into public spaces all over the country to the delight of audiences. While this was a wonderful conclusion to a Season at the Royal Opera House, no sooner had the curtain come down on the final night than suitcases were being packed for the Company's annual tour, this time to Japan and Spain. It has been a busy, exciting and demanding Season, with the challenging mixture of the familiar and the new that keeps The Royal Ballet on its world-class toes and reminds audiences that ballet is a wonderful and living art.

9

Miyako Yoshida

After 16 years dancing with the Company, Royal Ballet
Guest Principal Miyako Yoshida left the Company at the
end of the Season, dancing her last Cinderella on the main
stage and her last Juliet on tour. Her friend Sir Peter Wright
remembers her career to mark the occasion.

Before Miyako joined The Royal Ballet as a Principal in
1995 she had been a member of Sadler's Wells Royal Ballet
(now Birmingham Royal Ballet) for ten years, becoming
a Principal there in 1988. She was the most wonderful
and unassuming ballerina imaginable and adored by the
Birmingham public who, when she left, begged me to bring
her back whenever possible. Prior to joining BRB she had
spent two years at The Royal Ballet School refining her
already beautiful style and technique. It was there, at a
demonstration class attended by Dame Ninette de Valois,
that I first saw her. The class ended with the dreaded
32 *fouettés* and each of the girls had to execute them
separately. When it came to Miyako's turn she performed
them in such a perfect and effortless manner that Dame
Ninette interrupted the class and, turning to the audience
of teachers, said 'I have never seen this series of fiendishly
difficult turns executed so beautifully. It was sheer poetry
of movement', and turning to Miyako said, 'Thank you my
dear. You will go far!'

Although the rest is history and Miyako went on to
become one of our greatest ballerinas, she actually had a
very difficult start to her career. I had begged to have her
in my company (SWRB) and everyone agreed that she was
just what the company needed; someone with beautiful
classical line, style, elevation and a virtuoso technique,
although it would take time to develop her into the great
ballerina and artist that she was to become. Sadly, before
she joined us, she sustained an injury in her left ankle and I
was warned by her teachers that it might take a long time

to cure; and it did. However, I felt her talent was so special that I kept her place open, and finally – after six months – she was ready to start training properly. It was not long before she was dancing all those difficult Soloist roles in *Swan Lake* and *The Sleeping Beauty* and in such shorter ballets as *Les Rendezvous*, *Les Patineurs* and *Concerto*. And it was quite soon after that David Bintley decided to give her the leading role in his new version of *Sylvia*. At that time we were doing big tours of North and South America, Japan and the Far East where she started to dance most of the big Principal roles, getting continuity of performance and stamina. It was in Hong Kong that she really achieved the breakthrough into a fully fledged ballerina when she danced Odette/Odile for the first time. She always found it hard to express deep emotion and passion, essential for this role. Rehearsals were becoming very tense; we even had tears! But I knew I had to push her to the extent of her running out of rehearsal exclaiming, 'Peter Wright – he hate me!' How far from the truth can you get! But it did the trick and she was to give the most moving and technically perfect performances I had seen for a long while. It goes without saying that the 32 *fouettés* were magnificent!

The effortless way in which Miyako dances can be misleading. In fact she puts a huge amount of energy and effort into every step, turn or jump in order to make it look so wonderfully natural and easy. This was very much part of her early Japanese training. However, when Pat Neary put on *Theme and Variations* for SWRB it took some doing to get Miyako to make it look as if there was an element of danger about it – it all looked too easy! But in the end it all worked wonderfully, and she and Petter Jacobsson had the most phenomenal success in this great ballet. The excitement, both on stage and in the audience, was extraordinary.

I knew the time would come when she would need to make a change from this endless touring, and I dreaded it. Her example had raised the whole level of classical standards in BRB, particularly in such roles as the Sugar Plum Fairy and Aurora. But she had spent ten years with us, and understandably felt she really needed to 'settle' in one place and work consistently without the stress and strain of constant travelling.

Anthony Dowell, then Director of The Royal Ballet had always adored her and was keen to have her in the Company but she, on the other hand, was also being drawn to the idea of returning to Japan where she had become well known through her appearances there with BRB and her many visits as a Guest Artist with different Japanese companies. We had many discussions and, thank goodness, she accepted Anthony's offer. It was a terrible loss for BRB but for The Royal Ballet it has meant she would dance with the Company for 16 years, during which time she has become one of the most highly respected and much-loved Prima Ballerinas with a huge worldwide following. Her range is amazing and I believe she has chosen just the right moment to retire from dancing with the Company. She still looks wonderfully youthful, her technique and beautiful light jump are undiminished and, above all, her dance quality is as ravishing as ever. This is how she will always be remembered.

Dear Miyako, thank you for making Madam's prediction come true!

Sir Peter Wright CBE

Ivan Putrov

Principal Ivan Putrov also left The Royal Ballet at the end of the last Season having danced with the Company for 12 years, working with many of the most talented people in theatre and ballet, from dancers to répétiteurs and coaches. Working with Miyako Yoshida, for example, has been a pleasure for him. 'Miyako is always ready to give

her time to a young dancer... to allow them to develop as an artist, and I'm very grateful to her for that. I've danced many memorable shows with her including my first *Swan Lake*!'

'With Alexander Agadzhanov I've prepared all of the classical rep for many years, and with Patricia Neary I felt as if I was learning first hand from Balanchine! It is so inspiring to work with her, and I'm incredibly grateful that she has spent so much time with me on many roles including *Prodigal Son, Apollo, Agon* and others.'

Ivan is proud to have worked with Anthony Dowell, who invited him to join the Company in 1998. 'Sir Anthony has been a huge influence on me; he was my first Director and I have danced many roles that were created on him – Des Grieux in *Manon*, Boy with Matted Hair in *Shadowplay*,

Beliaev in *A Month in the Country* – so it is so valuable to have been coached by him. He is passing on his wisdom and knowledge, which for me is what really is the essence of The Royal Ballet, and it's a large part of why I joined the Company.'

Promoted to Principal after a few Seasons, Ivan has enjoyed the support of the many different people in different departments at the Royal Opera House. 'They are a great support to artists: people like Oliver Greatrex, in Costume Support, who on many occasions has been superb, even during performances, when you need someone to keep you going.'

Ivan is philosophical about the role of a dancer and the role of dance in the arts in general. 'For me, dance is just one form of expression, and it's so important to see other forms – it brings so much to my dancing.' For example he saw Massenet's *Manon,* one of the operas to finish off the Royal Opera Season with Anna Netrebko as Manon, and Vittorio Grigolo as her Des Grieux, the role Ivan danced in MacMillan's ballet. 'Grigolo was expressing the same story through singing that I expressed through dance.'

Ivan is foremost an artist and a lover of the arts. He quotes Stanislavsky, the Russian theater actor/director on dramatic method: 'Love the art in yourself and not yourself in the art.'

Viacheslav Samodurov

Viacheslav Samodurov (or Slava, as his many friends know him – indeed he has certainly endeared himself to everyone he has worked with, by all accounts) was a Principal with the Mariinsky Ballet and Dutch National Ballet before joining The Royal Ballet as Principal in 2003. He leaves the Company at the end of the 2009/10 Season to pursue a career as a choreographer: 'I'm only quitting dance as a dancer!', he reassures us.

Since dancing with the Company (having been already familiar with most of the classics when he arrived) Slava has absorbed the work, repertory and inspiration, and all have shaped his own style and taste. 'The Company has shaped a lot of what is in me now and it will always be a part of what I do. My understanding of ballet in general, of the way choreography should be approached and expressed, the way something should be performed, has been shaped by my experience here.' And it is for the influences of people such as Royal Ballet Resident Choreographer Wayne McGregor that he feels most grateful. 'Though I've never worked with Wayne, his presence and encouragement and the fact that he's always open to talk about ballet and choreography, has been a great inspiration. I don't think I would be setting out in this new direction without that.'

He very much admires his fellow dancers and will miss dancing with them: 'I've especially enjoyed my partnership with Sarah Lamb – I think we're definitely on the same page, and we're both insane workaholics!' But he has also taken great pleasure in working with the dancers as a choreographer which, he says, 'gives you another chance to realize what special people you're working with'. Over the last few Seasons, the New Works programme in the Linbury Studio Theatre has given him opportunities to create choreography on some of the Company's dancers. Mara Galeazzi has danced in the last two pieces he created for the Linbury – *Nonlinear Interactions* in 2009 and *Trip Trac* in 2010, which he set to Shostakovich piano Preludes and Fugues. 'I really enjoyed working with Mara. When you choreograph on your colleagues you learn a great deal from a different perspective and you have the chance to see their receptiveness, professionalism and dedication in ways that are not immediately obvious.'

After seeing Slava's *Trip Trac*, Sarah Crompton in the *Daily Telegraph* wrote that as a choreographer he 'looks

ready to fly'. And Slava, just back in London after creating a new piece on the Mikhailovsky, called *In a Minor Key*, adds: 'I will certainly be flying over new territories.'

Henry Roche

Henry Roche retired as Head of Music Staff at the end of the Season, after 33 years playing piano for ballet rehearsals and class, managing the busy schedule of the Company's music staff and playing in performance. While studying at the RCM in 1970, Henry met David Parkhouse who suggested Henry play for students at the Royal Academy of Dance to pay for his post-graduate lessons. And in 1977 Henry joined the music staff of The Royal Ballet.

13

This page: Henry Roche, who retired as Head of Music Staff at the end of the 2009/10 Season

Photograph: Rob Moore

'For me ballet was the best thing to get into; the music is always wonderful. But you need the experience to know what playing for ballet rehearsals is all about.' He remembers playing for Pat Neary's rehearsals with the Company (such as for *Symphony in C* last Season): 'She doesn't say things like "third movement", but just starts singing the tune and says "and one…", and you have to know where to pick it up.' The view from the rehearsal studio is very different from what happens on stage. 'One of the joys of playing a stage-and-piano full call is the cumulative musical effect. In rehearsal we wouldn't normally play the march from the beginning of *The Sleeping Beauty*, for example, but only when it's all put together on stage. The music makes sense then, much like doing a performance.' But he has grown to love the stopping and starting of the studio pianist: 'it's so nice to play and watch the dancers reacting.' There is something very special about rehearsals for Henry and he fondly remembers the various répétiteurs for whom he's played.

'Monica [Mason] is lovely to work with. She has a wonderful memory and knows the ballets inside out, and often teaches from a musician's point of view – as the pianist you really feel a part of what she's doing. And Christopher Carr takes full calls from 4.30pm to 6.30pm, keeping everyone entertained and timed to perfection, he always finishes right on time. He's very easy to play for. Both Johnny [Cope] and Lesley [Collier] started in The Royal Ballet, and both seem to have the ability to get right to the heart of the choreography and bring out what's best for the individual dancers.'

He is not only grateful to his team of rehearsal pianists for their work in the studios, but also on occasions for saving his life! 'I tend to get quite excited on tour because of the sheer joy of travelling. Paul Stobart once stepped in when I started arguing with armed Korean Soldiers, and Philip Cornfield was the voice of reason when I was about to do a U-turn in a busy street in San Francisco!'

14

The Company

He has very much enjoyed working as a performer too. When Johan Kobborg choreographed *Les Lutins* for the Linbury Studio Theatre, to a Caprice by Wieniawski and Bazzini's 'La Ronde des Lutins', Charlie Siem played the virtuoso violin part, which is very fast, but for Henry on piano it was also demanding to keep up. 'When we did it in Cuba it wasn't possible to have the piano on stage, but the violinist has to be because the dancer [Alina Cojocaru] refers to him at the end. So I couldn't see him, and there was so much laughter from the audience that I couldn't really hear him either. I just waited until I could hear and then joined in!' When the Company dedicated a memorial to its founders at Westminster Abbey, Henry played piano for Romany Pajdak who danced Ashton's 'Wise Virgin' solo, a solo that Fonteyn had danced. 'As soon as she started dancing it made the music twice as beautiful. Ashton has added a dimension to something already beautiful. And that's what I love about playing for ballet – the dancing makes the music something more than it was before. Without ballet I would never have learned how to make the piano sing. At the highest level, where the dancing is really beautiful, it's a challenge to make the music beautiful enough.'

Henry will miss being in the studio, playing for the dancers. 'It's a wonderful job, but it will also be wonderful having more free time. I'm very interested in genealogy and someone's writing a book about my great-great-grandfather [the composer Ignaz Moscheles], so I will have more time to help with their research. I have amassed a card index for 25 years, since I went to Brazil in 1984!'

And I do want to travel a bit and see friends and relatives I've had so little time to see! Now, if people invite me to a wedding on the other side of the world, I shall have to go – I won't have the excuse of being at work!'

Entrances and Exits

During the 2009/10 Season

At the end of the Season, Guest Principal Miyako Yoshida and Principals Slava Samodurov and Ivan Putrov left the Company. First Soloist Yohei Sasaki, Soloist Gemma Sykes, First Artists Cindy Jourdain, Ernst Meisner and Richard Ramsey, and Artist Xander Parish, all left the Company.

Assistant Ballet Master Gary Avis became Ballet Master. Henry Roche retired as Head of Music Staff and is replaced by Robert Clark. Tim Qualtrough also left the music staff, and Richard Coates joined it.

For the 2010/11 Season

First Soloist Sergei Polunin is promoted to Principal. Soloist Johannes Stepanek is promoted to First Soloist, First Artist Melissa Hamilton is promoted to Soloist and Artists Claire Calvert, Akane Takada, Fernando Montaño and Erico Montes are all promoted to First Artists.

Nehemiah Kish joins the Company as Principal from the Royal Danish Ballet and Itziar Mendizabal from the Leipzig Ballet joins as a First Soloist. Graduates from The Royal Ballet School Yasmine Naghdi, Sander Blommaert and James Butcher join the Company as Artists, as do Valentino Zucchetti from the Norwegian Ballet (and who trained at The Royal Ballet School), Camille Bracher from Johannesburg, South Africa and Beatriz Stix-Brunell from the School of American Ballet.

Season Images
Looking Back at 2009/10

Mayerling
Ballet in three acts

Music
Franz Liszt *arranged and orchestrated by* John Lanchbery

Choreography
Kenneth MacMillan

Designs
Nicholas Georgiadis

Scenario
Gillian Freeman

Lighting design
John B. Read

Staging
Grant Coyle, Monica Mason, Monica Parker

Ballet Master
Christopher Saunders

Ballet Mistress
Ursula Hageli

Principal coaching
Lesley Collier, Jonathan Cope, Monica Parker, Georgina Parkinson, Irek Mukhamedov

Premiere: 14 February 1978 (The Royal Ballet)

Mayerling
(October, November)

This page

Top: Rupert Pennefather as Crown Prince Rudolf in *Mayerling*

Bottom left: Melissa Hamilton as Mary Vetsera in *Mayerling*

Middle: Mara Galeazzi as Mary Vetsera in *Mayerling*

Bottom right: Mara Galeazzi as Mary Vetsera and Edward Watson as Crown Prince Rudolf in *Mayerling*

Photographs: Bill Cooper

16

The Sleeping Beauty
Ballet in a prologue and three acts

Music
Pyotr Il'yich Tchaikovsky
Choreography
Marius Petipa
Additional choreography
Frederick Ashton,
Anthony Dowell,
Christopher Wheeldon

Production
Monica Mason and
Christopher Newton
after Ninette de Valois
and Nicholas Sergeyev
Original designs
Oliver Messel
Realization and additional designs
Peter Farmer
Lighting design
Mark Jonathan
Staging
Christopher Carr
Ballet Mistress
Ursula Hageli
Principal coaching
Alexander Agadzhanov,
Lesley Collier, Roland
Price

Premieres: 3 January
1890 (Mariinsky Theatre,
St Petersburg);
2 February 1939
(The Royal Ballet)

**The Sleeping Beauty
(October, November)**
This page
Top: Prologue: Helen
Crawford as the Lilac
Fairy in *The Sleeping
Beauty*

Bottom left: Sergei
Polunin as Prince
Florimund in *The
Sleeping Beauty*

Bottom right:
Hikaru Kobayashi as
Princess Aurora in
The Sleeping Beauty

Photographs:
Johan Persson

17

Agon

Music
Igor Stravinsky

Choreography
George Balanchine

Lighting design
John B. Read

Staging
Patricia Neary

Ballet Master
Christopher Saunders

Premieres: 1 December
1957 (New York City
Ballet); 25 January 1973
(The Royal Ballet)

**Mixed Programme
(November)**

This page:
Ivan Putrov in *Agon*

Opposite page:
Edward Watson as
Anubis in *Sphinx*

Photographs:
Bill Cooper

18

Sphinx

Music
Bohuslav Martinů
Choreography
Glen Tetley

Set designs
Rouben Ter-Arutunian
Costume designs
Willa Kim
Lighting design
John B. Read
Staging
Bronwen Curry
Ballet Mistress
Ursula Hageli

Premieres: 9 December
1977 (American Ballet
Theatre); 4 November
2009 (The Royal Ballet)

Limen

Music
Kaija Saariaho
Choreography
Wayne McGregor

Set and video design
Tatsuo Miyajima
Costume designs
Moritz Junge
Lighting design
Lucy Carter
Assistant Ballet Master
Gary Avis
Dance Notator
Anna Trevien

Premiere: 4 November
2009 (The Royal Ballet)

**Mixed Programme
(November)**

This page: Sarah
Lamb and Eric
Underwood in *Limen*

Opposite page:
Mara Galeazzi and
Paul Kay in *Limen*

Photographs: Bill
Cooper

20

The Nutcracker
Ballet in two acts

Music
Pyotr Il'yich Tchaikovsky

Choreography
Peter Wright after Lev Ivanov

Original scenario
Marius Petipa
after E.T.A. Hoffmann's *Nussknacker und Mausekönig*

Production and scenario
Peter Wright

Designs
Julia Trevelyan Oman

Lighting design
Mark Henderson

Production consultant
Roland John Wiley

Staging
Christopher Carr

Ballet Mistress
Ursula Hageli

Principal coaching
Alexander Agadzhanov, Gary Avis, Lesley Collier, Jonathan Cope, Roland Price, Christopher Saunders

Dance Notators
Grant Coyle, Anna Trevien

Premieres: 18 December 1892 (Mariinsky Theatre, St Petersburg); 20 December 1984 (The Royal Ballet, this production); 17 December 1999 (revisions to this production)

22

Tales of Beatrix Potter

Music
John Lanchbery
Choreography
Frederick Ashton

Production
Anthony Dowell
Designs
Christine Edzard
Masks
Rostislav Doboujinsky
Lighting design
Mark Jonathan

Premiere: 4 December 1992 (The Royal Ballet)

Mixed Programme (December, January)

This page

Top: Kenta Kura as Mr Jeremy Fisher in *Tales of Beatrix Potter*

Bottom: Samantha Raine as Jemima Puddle Duck and Gary Avis as the Fox in *Tales of Beatrix Potter*

Photographs: Tristram Kenton

The Nutcracker (November - January)

Opposite page

Top: Iohna Loots as Clara in the Dance of the Mirlitons

Bottom right: Iohna Loots as Clara and Ricardo Cervera as Hans-Peter/Nutcracker

Bottom left: Olivia Cowley and Xander Parish in the Arabian Dance

Photographs: Johan Persson

23

Les Patineurs

Music
Giacomo Meyerbeer
arranged by Constant
Lambert
Choreography
Frederick Ashton

Designs
William Chappell
Lighting design
John B. Read
Staging
Christopher Carr, Grant
Coyle
Ballet Mistress
Ursula Hageli
Principal coaching
Gary Avis, Jonathan Cope

Premiere: 16 February
1937 (Vic-Wells Ballet)

**Mixed Programme
(December, January)**

The four Brown
Couples in *Les
Patineurs*

Photograph: Tristram
Kenton

24

Royal Ballet
Yearbook 2010/11

26

Romeo and Juliet
Ballet in three acts

Music
Sergey Prokofiev
Choreography
Kenneth MacMillan

Designs
Nicholas Georgiadis
Lighting design
John B. Read
Staging
Monica Mason
Ballet Masters
Christopher Saunders
Ballet Mistress
Ursula Hageli
Principal coaching
Alexander Agadzhanov,
Lesley Collier, Jonathan
Cope, Monica Mason

Premiere: 9 February
1965 (The Royal Ballet)

**Romeo and Juliet
(January – March)**
Opposite page: Sarah
Lamb as Juliet
This page: Bennet
Gartside as Tybalt
Photographs: Johan
Persson

27

As One

Music
Graham Fitkin

Choreography
Jonathan Watkins

Set design
Simon Daw

Costume designs
Vicki Mortimer

Lighting design
Neil Austin

Video design
Simon Daw and Tim Reid

Ballet Master
Christopher Saunders

Premiere: 19 February
2010 (The Royal Ballet)

**Mixed Programme
(February, March)**

This page: Steven
McRae in *As One*

Opposite page

Top: Laura Morera
and Edward Watson
in *As One*

Bottom: Edward
Watson, Kristen
McNally, Eric
Underwood, Steven
McRae, Laura
Morera and Thomas
Whitehead in *As One*

Photographs:
Bill Cooper

28

**Rushes: Fragments
of a Lost Story**

Music
Sergey Prokofiev
*arranged and elaborated
by* Michael Berkeley
Choreography
Kim Brandstrup

Designs
Richard Hudson
Lighting design
Jean Kalman
Video design
Dick Straker
*Assistant to the
Choreographer*
Deirdre Chapman

Premiere: 23 April 2008
(The Royal Ballet)

**Mixed Programme
(February, March)**

This page: Laura
Morera and Carlos
Acosta in *Rushes:
Fragments of a Lost
Story*

Opposite page: Sarah
Lamb and Marianela
Nuñez in *Infra*

Photographs:
Bill Cooper

30

Infra

Music
Max Richter
Choreography
Wayne McGregor

Set designs
Julian Opie
Costume designs
Moritz Junge
Lighting design
Lucy Carter
Sound design
Chris Ekers
Ballet Master
Gary Avis

Premiere: 13 November
2008 (The Royal Ballet)

La Fille mal gardée
(The Wayward Daughter)
Ballet in two acts

Music
Ferdinand Hérold
arranged and orchestrated by John Lanchbery
Choreography
Frederick Ashton
Scenario
Jean Dauberval

Designs
Osbert Lancaster
Lighting design
John B. Read
Staging
Alexander Grant
assisted by Christopher Carr, Grant Coyle
Ballet Mistress
Ursula Hageli
Ballet Master
Gary Avis
Principal coaching
Alexander Agadzhanov, Lesley Collier, Roland Price, Christopher Saunders

Premiere: 28 January 1960 (The Royal Ballet)

La Fille mal gardée (March, April)

This page: Philip Mosley as Widow Simone and members of the corps de ballet

Photograph: Tristram Kenton

32

The Judas Tree

Music
Brian Elias
Choreography
Kenneth MacMillan

Designs
Jock McFadyen
Lighting design
Mark Henderson
Staging
Karl Burnett
Principal coaching
Jonathan Cope, Irek Mukhamedov

Premiere: 19 March 1993
(The Royal Ballet)

The Judas Tree

This page

Top left: José Martín, Eric Underwood and Leanne Benjamin in *The Judas Tree*

Right: Carlos Acosta and Leanne Benjamin *The Judas Tree*

Bottom Left: José Martín and Thomas Whitehead in *The Judas Tree*

Photographs: Johan Persson

33

Concerto

Music
Dmitry Shostakovich
Choreography
Kenneth MacMillan

Designs
Jürgen Rose
Lighting design
John B. Read
Staging
Christopher Carr
Ballet Mistress
Ursula Hageli
Principal coaching
Gary Avis, Christopher
Carr, Lesley Collier,
Monica Mason
Dance Notator
Grant Coyle

Premieres: 30 November
1966 (Berliner Ballett);
26 May 1967 (The Royal
Ballet)

**Mixed Programme
(March, April)**

This page: Yuhui
Choe in *Concerto*

Opposite page: Sarah
Lamb and Ryoichi
Hirano in *Concerto*

Photographs: Johan
Persson

34

35

Elite Syncopations

Music
Scott Joplin and other
Ragtime composers

Choreography
Kenneth MacMillan

Costume designs
Ian Spurling

Lighting design
John B. Read

Staging
Julie Lincoln

Ballet Master
Christopher Saunders

Premiere: 7 October 1974
(The Royal Ballet)

**Mixed Programme
(March, April)**

This page

Left: Mara Galeazzi in
Elite Syncopations

Right: Jonathan
Watkins in *Elite
Syncopations*

Photographs: Johan
Persson

36

Cinderella
Ballet in three acts

Music
Sergey Prokofiev
Choreography
Frederick Ashton

Production, Director and Supervisor
Wendy Ellis Somes
Set designs
Toer van Schayk
Costume designs
Christine Haworth
Lighting design
Mark Jonathan
Staging
Christopher Carr
Ballet Mistress
Ursula Hageli
Ballet Master
Gary Avis
Principal coaching
Alexander Agadzhanov, Lesley Collier, Jonathan Cope, Roland Price, Wendy Ellis Somes
Dance Notator
Grant Coyle

Premiere: 23 December 1948 (The Royal Ballet)

Cinderella
(April - June)
This page: Roberta Marquez as Cinderella and Steven McRae as the Prince in *Cinderella*

Photograph: Tristram Kenton

37

Electric Counterpoint

Music
J.S. Bach, Steve Reich
Choreography
Christopher Wheeldon

Designs
Jean Marc Puissant
Lighting design
Natasha Chivers
Video Artists
Michael Nunn, William Trevitt
Sound design
Mukul Patel
Ballet Master
Christopher Saunders
Dance Notator
Anna Trevien

Premiere: 28 February 2008 (The Royal Ballet)

Mixed Programme (May)

This page

Left: Sergei Polunin in *Electric Counterpoint*

Right: Marianela Nuñez in *Electric Counterpoint*

Opposite page: Gary Avis in *Carmen*

Photographs: Johan Persson

38

Carmen

Music
Georges Bizet *arranged by* Rodion Shchedrin
Choreography
Mats Ek

Designs
Marie Louise Ekman
Lighting design
Jörgen Jansson
Staging
Pompea Santoro,
Veli–Pekka Peltokallio
Principal coaching
Pompea Santoro,
Veli–Pekka Peltokallio
Dance Notator
Mayumi Hotta

Premieres: 13 May 1992
(Cullberg Ballet); 10 April
2002 (The Royal Ballet)

39

40

Asphodel Meadows

Music
Francis Poulenc
Choreography
Liam Scarlett

Designs
John Macfarlane
Lighting
Jennifer Tipton
Ballet Master
Gary Avis
Dance Notator
Amanda Eyles

Premiere: 5 May 2010
(The Royal Ballet)

**Mixed Programme
(May)**
Opposite page:
Marianela Nuñez and
Rupert Pennefather
in *Asphodel
Meadows*

This page: Leanne
Cope in *Asphodel
Meadows*
Photographs:
Johan Persson

41

Chroma

Music
Joby Talbot, Jack
White III,
arranged by Joby
Talbot, *orchestrated by*
Christopher Austin
Choreography
Wayne McGregor

Set designs
John Pawson
Costume designs
Moritz Junge
Lighting design
Lucy Carter
Ballet Master
Gary Avis

Premiere: 17 November
2006 (The Royal Ballet)

**Mixed Programme
(April - June)**

This page

Top left: Melissa
Hamilton in *Chroma*

Top right: Samantha
Raine in *Chroma*

Bottom left:
Olivia Cowley and
Johannes Stepanek
in *Chroma*

Bottom right: Dawid
Trzensimiech in
Chroma

Opposite page:
Hikaru Kobayashi
and Bennet Gartside,
Sarah Lamb and
Steven McRae,
Samantha Raine
and Valeri Hristov in
Symphony in C

Photographs:
Bill Cooper

42

Symphony in C

Music
Georges Bizet
Choreography
George Balanchine

Designs
Anthony Dowell
Lighting design
John B. Read
Staging
Patricia Neary
Ballet Master
Christopher Saunders
Dance Notator
Anna Trevien

Premieres: 28 July 1947
(Paris Opéra Ballet);
20 November 1991
(The Royal Ballet)

Tryst

Music
James MacMillan
Choreography
Christopher Wheeldon

Designs
Jean-Marc Puissant
Lighting design
Natasha Katz
Ballet Master
Christopher Saunders

Premiere: 18 May 2002
(The Royal Ballet)

**Mixed Programme
(April - June)**

This page: Ricardo
Cervera and
Samantha Raine

Opposite page: the
corps de ballet in
Tryst

Photographs:
Bill Cooper

44

45

The Company Abroad

by Zoë Anderson

Ballet is an international art form. Across the world, there's a constant exchange of dancers, of ballets, of training and influence. To see how cosmopolitan ballet has become, just look at the last programme of the Royal Ballet's 2009/10 Season. Each of those performances of three short ballets ended with Balanchine's *Symphony in C* – a sunburst celebration of classical dancing, created for a French company by a Russian-American choreographer. On opening night, The Royal Ballet cast was led by American Sarah Lamb, Australian Steven McRae, Argentinian Marianela Nuñez, British Rupert Pennefather and Edward Watson, Japanese Yuhui Choe, Ukrainian Sergei Polunin and Spanish Laura Morera. Many of those dancers trained at The Royal Ballet School; others came to this Company as adults, drawn by its reputation and repertory. That same mixed programme included Christopher Wheeldon's *Tryst* and Wayne McGregor's *Chroma* – one work by a choreographer who grew up in The Royal Ballet, the other by its Resident Choreographer, both in demand around the world. The Company's reach is global.

So are its working methods. For instance, Wheeldon's latest ballet for the Company, *Alice's Adventures in Wonderland*, is a co-production with the National Ballet of Canada. *Alice* is to be a substantial new production: an evening-length work, with a commissioned score by Joby Talbot. Lewis Carroll's famous story offers spectacular visual opportunities, from the landscapes of Wonderland to its weird and eccentric inhabitants. Wheeldon has said that these characters 'cry out for movement – it's a very physical story, which was what attracted me'. The range and fantasy of the story means that the designs, by the award-winning Bob Crowley, are likely to be complex. Crowley and Wheeldon are drawing on Tenniel's famous illustrations, but they're also looking at Carroll's own photography. Wheeldon plans to use animated projections to carry out the story's magical effects. *Alice* is not a small or simple production; this is a big, ambitious undertaking.

Making the ballet as a co-production gives both companies access to a new work, while boosting the budget needed for such an elaborate commission. Wheeldon is creating the new ballet in Britain, making his roles for the dancers of The Royal Ballet – he's suggested that Steven McRae's skills as a tap dancer may find their way into the role of the Mad Hatter. The world premiere takes place in London in February 2011 – and then the production heads abroad, with the Canadian premiere following in June. Within months, Wheeldon's new *Alice* will be seen on two continents.

Similarly, the re-creation of Frederick Ashton's *Sylvia*, which returns in autumn 2010, was a co-production between The Royal Ballet and American Ballet Theatre. Created in 1952 to show off Ashton's muse, the ballerina Margot Fonteyn, *Sylvia* had not lasted long in the repertory after Fonteyn stopped dancing it. Yet this was a full-length work by one of The Royal Ballet's defining choreographers, a fond evocation of 19th-century ballet spectacle with a sumptuous Delibes score and a virtuoso ballerina role. There was real interest in rediscovering it – not just within The Royal Ballet, where the work is part of Company history, but from the international ballet world. As with Wheeldon's *Alice*, the work on the new *Sylvia* production took place in London, drawing on Royal Ballet memories and expertise. After its British premiere it went on to America, where it was promoted as an example of the 'English school' of ballet, showing off the speedy footwork and melting upper body movement for which Ashton's choreography and The Royal Ballet dancers were famous. *Sylvia* has now been passed on to a new generation of dancers and audiences, on both sides of the Atlantic. Since its British premiere it has also been performed in Berlin and Tokyo.

Both those partner companies, American Ballet Theatre and the National Ballet of Canada, have a shared past with

The Royal Ballet. The British company, founded in 1931 by Ninette de Valois, has had an inspiring influence on world ballet. Lucia Chase, the founding patron of ABT, took the Sadler's Wells Ballet (as The Royal Ballet used to be called) as one of her models. For the National Ballet of Canada, the links were even stronger. It was De Valois who had recommended the company's first director, former Sadler's Wells dancer Celia Franca. The Royal Ballet's touring carried its distinctive vision of ballet around the world. The Company's staff have often stayed longer abroad, taking a direct hand in setting up, encouraging and maintaining companies in other countries.

Of course, ballet's internationalism has been around for centuries. Celebrated dancers have always travelled, dazzling foreign cities and spreading interest in their art form. The Royal Ballet itself is one of a wave of companies that sprang up under the influence of Diaghilev's Ballets Russes. From 1909 until Diaghilev's death in 1929, this spectacular company revolutionized theatre dance, introducing Western audiences to dancers such as Nijinsky and Karsavina, choreographers such as Fokine, Nijinska and Balanchine, composers such as Stravinsky and Prokofiev. Ninette de Valois danced with the Ballets Russes from 1923 until 1925, when she left to found her own company. 'I saw the whole of theatre in relation to the ballet', she remembered. 'They had this heritage behind them... the classwork was impeccable, and then we had these ballets and these marvellous choreographers. I just had everything on a plate. What could I do but stand and sort it out like a jigsaw puzzle, and realize that we had absolutely nothing in England, and all I wanted to do was to get back and start something.' She did; and her own company, inspired by Diaghilev, was soon inspiring its own descendents.

Though De Valois learned much from the Ballets Russes, her own company would be run on very different lines. The Ballets Russes had been a touring international troupe, an exotic visitor to the cities of the world. De Valois wanted a national company, firmly grounded with its own school. Yet her ambitions were global: she was thinking on an international scale from very early on. The Vic-Wells Ballet, as it was then called, gave its first full evening performance in 1931. The next year, it gave its first overseas performance, at a trade exhibition in Copenhagen. 'Australia and South Africa are anxious for a visit', De Valois would write in 1938, already eyeing the prospect of a world tour.

Large-scale overseas touring would have to wait, delayed by the outbreak of World War II. The Sadler's Wells Ballet did make propaganda visits abroad. One terrifying trip took them to the Netherlands in 1940, where they were caught up in the Nazi invasion of the country. The dancers escaped, abandoning sets and costumes, making it back to Britain in the hold of a cargo ship. Back home, they performed tirelessly in London and across the country. Ballet, which had been a fairly specialist interest in the 1930s, achieved a new, widespread popularity. Audience demand was so high that at one point the company gave three shows a day – though this schedule had to be abandoned when exhausted corps de ballet girls started fainting on stage. By the end of the war, the Sadler's Wells Ballet had become a much-loved institution, with national stars in Margot Fonteyn and Robert Helpmann.

That status was recognized in the Company's move to the Royal Opera House after the war. In 1946, the theatre reopened with the iconic Oliver Messel production of *The Sleeping Beauty*. De Valois set up a second, touring

48

branch of the Company at Sadler's Wells, its own home theatre. Astonishingly, she also found time to set up a third company in 1946 – not at home, but in Turkey. In 1947, the Turkish government asked De Valois if she could found a national school of ballet in their country – a bold move, since Turkish audiences had little or no experience of the art form. De Valois didn't hesitate; she visited Istanbul and Ankara in 1947, and by January 1948 had set up the first Turkish vocational school. In nine years, this had trained enough students to start a performing company. By 1960, they were ready to stage their first production of a 19th-century ballet, *Coppélia*. Alongside the classics, De Valois encouraged Turkish choreography, leading by example. Her 1964 ballet *At the Fountainhead* drew on local dances and folklore, including a duet for two shadow puppets.

De Valois loved Turkey, keeping a fond interest in her overseas company. On one visit to Ankara, she arrived to find that her luggage had gone missing. 'It doesn't matter', she told Richard Glasstone, who became the Turkish company's resident choreographer in 1960. 'I've got the important things in my hand-luggage.' The 'important things' were two tutus and some pointe shoes.

While De Valois was setting up the Turkish troupe, she was pushing her British Company to international heights. In 1949, the Company made its world reputation overnight, on its first visit to North America. They danced *The Sleeping Beauty* at the Metropolitan Opera House, New York, with Fonteyn as Aurora. The reception 'surpassed anything that the Metropolitan has ever experienced', reported one critic, 'and there have been ovations at the opera house before Sadler's Wells arrived here'. The audience reaction was overwhelming. Kenneth MacMillan, who danced that night, remembered one man 'almost falling out of a box, he was so excited'. The magazines *Time* and *Newsweek* put Fonteyn on their front covers – in the 1940s, something usually reserved for political leaders. 'In four weeks', *Time* reported, 'Margot Fonteyn and Sadler's Wells had restored as much glitter to Britain's tarnished tiara as any mission the English had sent abroad since the war.'

The dancers and *The Sleeping Beauty* were a revelation, but so was the whole approach to ballet. *The Sleeping Beauty* and *Swan Lake*, now the staples of ballet repertory, were then rarely seen in the West. The De Valois company model – with a programme of new works, important ballets from other companies, a backbone of the 19th-century classics – has been so influential that it no longer looks radical. But at this point, most post-Diaghilev companies danced only excerpts of the 19th-century works: the second act of *Swan Lake*, the third act from *The Sleeping Beauty*. The Sadler's Wells Ballet presented the complete works, with a scale and confidence that audiences found intoxicating. In one bound, this company made its international name. The rest of the world was soon not just 'anxious for a visit', but clamouring. When, in 1956, Sadler's Wells became The Royal Ballet, it was the world's most influential company, admired throughout Europe, America and the British Commonwealth. Like the Ballets Russes, it had other companies springing up in its wake, inspired by these performances, this example.

In 1949, the transatlantic tour continued across the USA and on to Canada, with ecstatic audiences throughout. The new National Ballet of Canada, under Franca, gave its first performance in 1951. The Royal Ballet influence lasted: Franca was succeeded as director by Alexander Grant, another member of the British company.

Grant himself was born in New Zealand. The Company has always had an international cast, drawing dancers from overseas as well as Britain. Robert Helpmann, one of its

49

biggest early stars, came from Australia; Grant was one of a generation of dancers who headed for Britain after the war. When De Valois founded the Company, Britain still had an empire; its colonies and independent Dominions still felt strong links with Britain. Australian and Canadian dancers, seeking a ballet career, turned naturally to Britain, as did those from African countries. They were to include some of the Company's biggest stars: Nadia Nerina and Monica Mason from South Africa, Merle Park from what was then Rhodesia, Lynn Seymour from Canada. The political landscape has changed radically since then, but some family feeling remains. Steven McRae remembers that, in his early teens, he was surprised when his teacher urged him to aim for The Royal Ballet. 'I was like, "Is that Sydney or Melbourne? Why do I need to go to London?"' He soon came to agree with her.

In the 1950s and '60s, the links that drew dancers to Britain also made the Sadler's Wells organization the obvious model for companies being set up overseas. When an Australian national troupe was planned, like Canada, De Valois and her team were again the first source of advice. In 1959, De Valois suggested Peggy van Praagh, who had directed the touring company, as the new leader of Australia's Borovansky Ballet, which was soon reformed as the Australian Ballet. Helpmann later became her co-director – an Australian dancer, returning to his roots.

In some cases, then, The Royal Ballet has literally helped with the creation of other companies. It's also had a more general influence, as its dancers, choreographers and staff have worked around the world, taking Royal Ballet training, ballets and approaches with them. When Alexander Grant took over the National Ballet of Canada, he introduced several Ashton ballets to his new company's repertory. In 1966, Kenneth MacMillan was appointed director of the Berlin Ballet, where he stayed for three years. He created several new ballets for his Berlin company, but also added Ashton to its repertory, plus a new production of *The Sleeping Beauty* – in other words, he was spreading core Royal Ballet values. MacMillan would return to direct The Royal Ballet itself, from 1970 to 1977. In the 1980s, he would become artistic advisor to American Ballet Theatre – where, again, he staged another *The Sleeping Beauty*.

He also staged his own *Romeo and Juliet*, created for The Royal Ballet in 1965. There are plenty of *Romeo* ballets to Prokofiev's celebrated score, but MacMillan's has become the world's *Romeo*, a huge international hit, danced by The Royal Ballet and now by many other companies. This is The Royal Ballet's other form of international influence: the way its repertory, its own choreographers, have been taken up by other companies. The works of Ashton and MacMillan, the Company's two defining choreographers, are danced from America to Russia, from Australia to Japan. More recently, works created for the Company have entered international repertory. Just look back at the mixed programme that ended The Royal Ballet's 2009/10 Season, and at *Chroma* and *Tryst*, the two ballets that were given their premieres by this company. Christopher Wheeldon has just staged *Tryst* for Dutch National Ballet. McGregor's *Chroma* is appearing at the National Ballet of Canada in autumn 2010 and in 2011 will be re-staged for San Francisco Ballet and danced by the Bolshoi Ballet too. That final mixed programme of the Season showed an international stage – and its achievements, as in days gone by, are reflected on stages around the world.

Zoë Anderson is the author of *The Royal Ballet: 75 Years*, published by Faber & Faber in 2006

Capturing Movement

by Will Richmond

In the eight decades of The Royal Ballet's history, theatre photography has evolved tremendously. Ballet portraits have recorded the talents and personalities that have shaped the Company since its early years as it developed out of Ninette de Valois' Academy of Choreographic Art.

In the 1920s, '30s and '40s, theatre photographer Gordon Anthony, De Valois' brother, created classic images of performing arts celebrities from Cecil Beaton to Vivien Leigh and Lyn Redgrave, but also such Royal Ballet greats as Robert Helpmann, Frederick Ashton, Mikhail Fokine, Constant Lambert, Lilian Baylis and De Valois herself. All elegantly posed with Gordon's trademark deep shadows, his portraits beautifully capture the style and theatricality of these personalities, the facial expressions of the great

character dancers of the day and the poise and lines for which many of the Company's dancers are famed. From Markova and Dolin, to Helpmann and the young Fonteyn, Anthony documented some of the most famous dancers and partnerships in the Company's history. But the dance photographs – Markova on pointe, Fonteyn's inimicable *ports de bras* – were of necessity static, since shutter speeds of several seconds were sometimes required to account for low light. His Helpmann as Hamlet, for example, could just as well be performing a play as a ballet; his subjects frozen in movement to allow the photographer to get his picture.

It was only with such developments in technology as faster shutter speeds and more sensitive film that photography during actual performances was even possible. As with still photography of sports, ballet photography involves capturing fast movements in static frames of fractions of seconds. But the theatre is lit for the human eye. Ballet production designers manipulate the audience's perception through careful use of scenery and lights, creating atmosphere with darkness and shadows, mist and gauze, which is often very difficult to capture on film, and indeed even hinders getting a picture at all. The dream-like quality of the Shades in *La Bayadère* for example is enhanced through stage tricks including a gauze just behind the proscenium arch. This is subtle enough to be ignored by the audience but, when photographed, comes into relief, layering every picture with a vivid and detailed criss-cross effect not at all intended by the staging and which must be accommodated by the photographer. The vivid contrasts of blue-black painted drops behind dancers in pristine white long skirts in *Les Sylphides*, likewise requires the photographer to work hard to bring out the backdrop in its darkness at the same time as the dancers in their whiteness.

All these considerations make photographing ballet a tricky skill, and only the most accomplished photographers with the best equipment can capture the wonderful images you see of The Royal Ballet. Since dancers are no longer required to be motionless for their photographs, the photographer is required to know in detail which parts of their movements will make the best photograph.

Left: Alicia Markova as Giselle

Photograph: © Gordon Anthony/V&A Images/ V&A Theatre Collections

Johan Persson was a Principal dancer with The National Ballet of Canada and The Royal Ballet before becoming a photographer, and now regularly photographs the Company on stage and in rehearsal. Ballet photography today has come a long way since the early years of the Company, and photographers like Johan can only get the pictures we want to see by understanding both the art form they are photographing and the technology available to them.

Although the basics of dance photography have stayed the same, such as composition, lighting, focus and capturing the moment, technology plays an important part for the modern photographer and certainly images captured in live performances now weren't possible even ten years ago. The biggest change has been that from traditional film to digital capture. Digital cameras today are far more sensitive and produce a much cleaner and more detailed image than film was ever able to do, and this sensitivity is especially important in dance photography where often the light levels are low.

For the technique is very much about 'capturing the moment'. Classically trained ballet dancers know very well the shapes they mean to make with their bodies, and in the continuity of their fluid movements the 'moment' is often a brief glimpse. As Johan explains: 'My background as a dancer has been a great help when photographing dance. I understand the aesthetic of the art form, what the dancer is trying to achieve, and for me capturing the peak is instinctive.' The photographer can anticipate the *jeté*, for example, or closely follow the rise of a dancer's leg before the full *arabesque*. Many professional photographers speak of their automatic instinct to press the button a little before the shot needs to happen, to accommodate the

gap between pressing and the shutter functioning, or even between thinking to press and physically pressing, and in ballet photography this instinct is crucial to getting the right picture.

During the editing process I have a clear understanding of what is acceptable from the dancer's point of view in terms of line and placement. And it can also be a struggle not to limit oneself by these considerations. As the years pass, I find I'm less rigid and I'm drawn towards moments which capture the energy, movement or emotion of dance, even at the expense of the perfect line.

One of the great advantages of digital photography is that the photographer can take so many pictures at high speed and then select the frames that work best - which is a skill in iself - and without the constraints of film, this creates more opportunities for experiment. Deliberately slower shutter speeds, for example, can preserve the imperfections that ensure the signals of movement are not lost - the slight blur to the moving foot, or the wisp of hair as the dancer leaps through the air, allow us to understand, in a still image, the motion of the dancer 'frozen' in the flight of a *jeté*.

Capturing ballet in still photography is an art in itself and while its initial purpose might be to record the moments that punctuate a live performance it is also a way of savouring those brief, defining moments that are so memorable. In the final minutes of MacMillan's *Manon*, for example, the dying Manon leaps into the arms of her lover Des Grieux and as he grips her tightly she thrusts one arm into the air, reaching with the last efforts of her life, before he spins her around to face him and their *pas de deux* spirals to its tragic conclusion. There is one brief moment in which all the love, anguish, despair, living energy and dying fall that we have watched grow and change through the ballet, at once combine with Massenet's crescendo in the score. Only the greatest dancers can create that moment on stage and furthermore make it coincide with the music, but at the same time only the best photographers can capture it silently on camera. And when they do, the image becomes a lasting, concentrated memory of that final *pas de deux* and the emotions that have been channelled into it.

'Obviously a still image can't compete with the actual experience of watching live or filmed movement,' Johan concedes, 'but a still image can be far more powerful when a moment of emotion, line, and beauty are captured and a viewer is able to dwell on it.'

Of course the true experience will only happen in the auditorium but as technology moves on apace photography enables us to represent and remember something of that live wonder that makes ballet such an individual art form.

53

54

Onegin

Onegin
Ballet in three acts

Music
Kurt-Heinz Stolze
after Pyotr Il'yich
Tchaikovsky
Choreography
John Cranko

Previous pages:
Yolanda Sonnabend's
Fabergé inspired
set designs for
Swan Lake
Photograph:
Dee Conway

Christopher
Saunders as Doctor
Chebutykin in *Winter Dreams*
Photograph:
Bill Cooper

Federico Bonelli as
Des Grieux in *Manon*
Photograph:
Bill Cooper

David Makhatelli in
La Valse
Photograph:
Johan Persson

Alina Cojocaru as
Tatiana and Bennet
Gartside as Prince
Gremin in *Onegin*
Photograph:
Dee Conway

This page: Johan
Kobborg as Onegin
in *Onegin*
Photograph:
Dee Conway

Opposite page:
La Valse
Photograph:
Dee Conway

La Valse / New Brandstrup / Winter Dreams / Theme and Variations

Sylvia

Sylvia

Music
Léo Delibes

Choreography
Frederick Ashton

This page: Zenaida Yanowsky as Sylvia in *Sylvia*

Photograph: Bill Cooper

Opposite page

Top: Kenta Kura as the Jester in *Cinderella*

Bottom: Luke Heydon and Alastair Marriott as Cinderella's Step-Sisters

Photographs: Tristram Kenton

58

Cinderella

Cinderella

Music
Sergey Prokofiev

Choreography
Frederick Ashton

Production
Wendy Ellis Somes

Peter and the Wolf / Les Patineurs/ Tales of Beatrix Potter

Peter and the Wolf / Les Patineurs / Tales of Beatrix Potter

Peter and the Wolf

Music
Sergey Prokofiev

Choreography
Matthew Hart

Les Patineurs

Music
Giacomo Meyerbeer

Choreography
Frederick Ashton

Tales of Beatrix Potter

Music
John Lanchbery

Choreography
Frederick Ashton

Right: Dancers of The Royal Ballet in *Tales of Beatrix Potter*

Photograph: Tristram Kenton

60

Giselle

Giselle

Music
Adolphe Adam revised
by Joseph Horovitz
Choreography
Marius Petipa *after* Jean
Coralli and Jules Perrot

Left: Lauren
Cuthbertson as
Giselle

Photograph: Johan
Persson

Swan Lake

Swan Lake
Ballet in four acts

Music
Pyotr Il'yich Tchaikovsky
Choreography
Marius Petipa
and Lev Ivanov
Additional Choreography
Frederick Ashton
(Act III Neapolitan Dance)
and David Bintley
(Act I Waltz)

Production
Anthony Dowell

Right: Marianela
Nuñez as Odette and
Thiago Soares as
Prince Siegfried

Photograph:
Dee Conway

62

Alice's Adventures in Wonderland

Alice's Adventures in Wonderland

Music
Joby Talbot
Choreography
Christopher Wheeldon

Left: Principal Lauren Cuthbertson photographed in the Deanery Gardens of Christ Church, Oxford for the Royal Opera House Winter Season 2010/11 marketing. Lauren will be appearing in Christopher Wheeldon's *Alice's Adventures in Wonderland*

Photograph: Jason Bell

63

Rhapsody / Sensorium / 'Still Life' at the Penguin Café

Rhapsody / Sensorium / 'Still Life' at the Penguin Café

Rhapsody

Music
Sergey Rachmaninoff

Choreography
Frederick Ashton

Sensorium

Music
Claude Debussy *with orchestrations by* Colin Matthews

Choreography
Alastair Marriott

'Still Life' at the Penguin Café

Music
Simon Jeffes

Choreography
David Bintley

Top: Philip Broomhead as Southern Cape Zebra

Bottom: Dancers of The Royal Ballet as Penguins in *'Still Life' at the Penguin Café*

Photographs: Bill Cooper

64

APRIL/MAY/JUNE

Manon

Manon
Ballet in three acts

Music
Jules Massenet
*Orchestrated
and arranged by*
Leighton Lucas *with
the collaboration of*
Hilda Gaunt
Choreography
Kenneth MacMillan

Left: Tamara Rojo as Manon
Photograph:
Bill Cooper

65

Ballo della regina / New McGregor / DGV: Danse à grande vitesse

Ballo della regina / New McGregor / DGV: Danse à grande vitesse

Ballo della regina

Music
Giuseppe Verdi

Choreography
George Balanchine

New McGregor

Music
tbc

Choreography
Wayne McGregor

DGV: Danse à grande vitesse

Music
Michael Nyman

Choreography
Christopher Wheeldon

Right: Leanne Benjamin and Edward Watson in *DGV: Danse à grande vitesse*

Photograph: Johan Persson

66

Scènes de ballet / Voluntaries / The Rite of Spring

Scènes de ballet / Voluntaries / The Rite of Spring

Scènes de ballet

Music
Igor Stravinsky

Choreography
Frederick Ashton

Voluntaries

Music
Francis Poulenc

Choreography
Glen Tetley

The Rite of Spring

Music
Igor Stravinsky

Choreography
Kenneth MacMillan

Top: The Royal Ballet in *Voluntaries*
Photograph: Bill Cooper

Bottom: The Royal Ballet in *Scènes de ballet*
Photograph: Dee Conway

67

Portraits of De Valois

by Cristina Franchi

The 2010/11 Season includes the tenth anniversary of the death of the Founder of The Royal Ballet, Ninette de Valois – known to everyone as 'Madam'. She died on 8 March 2001 at the age of 102. The anniversary seemed an appropriate occasion to look back at her legacy, and among the events is a large exhibition mounted by Royal Opera House Collections in collaboration with The Lowry, Salford, from 23 October 2010 to 6 March 2011 and then at the Royal Opera House from 2 April into August 2011. The curator of the Exhibition, Cristina Franchi, talks about some of the many fascinating aspects of the life and character of one of the most inspirational, talented and influential figures of 20th-century ballet through items associated with the exhibition.

Ninette de Valois as a child, superscribed by her at a later date 'you never can tell! Tooty'. She was born Edris Stannus in Ireland in 1898 in Blessington in County Wicklow, Ireland (Tooty was her family nickname). She tells us in her biography, *Come Dance with Me,* that she had been taught to dance an Irish jig by the farmer's wife at the home farm of the estate her family owned. Even though she was a very shy child, at a party she suddenly announced that she wanted to do her Irish jig. She had some talent for dancing, which was encouraged when the family moved to England: she was given fancy dancing classes and then her mother enrolled her in Lila Field's dance academy to give her a professional training. She performed with the Lila Field Wonder Children, with whom she had to impersonate Pavlova in *The Dying Swan.* Her mother had taken her to see Pavlova at the Palace Theatre in London, and she learnt the dance by repeatedly going to the theatre, sitting in the gods and writing it down in a notebook. As a teenager she toured with the Lila Field company, putting together her own dances, looking after her costumes and shoes and sorting out her lodgings as they moved from one seaside town to another. Her early professional years are as far removed as you can imagine from that of a ballet dancer's career nowadays.

De Valois as a *premiére danseuse* in Verdi's *Aida* at the Royal Opera House (1919), superscribed by De Valois at a later date 'To Mollie – with love – from Edris'. Although she signed herself Edris, as a dancer she was by now calling herself professionally Ninette de Valois. What she considered her first professional engagement was as a dancer in the annual pantomime at the Lyceum Theatre, one of the two biggest pantomimes in London at that time. The shows had all sorts of stage effects and theatre styles, including clowns, an element of music hall and dancers. She performed in this for about four years and built up quite a following. In 1919 she came to the Royal Opera House for the first time and worked for Thomas Beecham and his Grand International Season of Opera; she performed as *première danseuse* for several seasons in all the different operas, including *Aida*. At this time there wasn't a British ballet company you could join – ballet was included as part of other theatre experiences. So, De Valois was dancing in opera, revues or even on a music hall bill. This gave her a sense of ballet as being one of the theatre arts rather than a separate art form, something she drew on for her own works.

A photograph of De Valois used in 1949 in the programme for *The Sleeping Beauty* at the Metropolitan Opera House, New York, during the Company's first tour to America. In many of her portraits she looks stern and forbidding, which is very much the director role. We have a letter in the exhibition written to Pauline Claydon, one of her dancers, as Claydon was leaving the Company, in which she writes: 'It is not often that anyone in my position can show or express any really personal pleasure that they may receive from an artist's performance. But some people make me forget to be "Madam".' So she was very much aware she had to be there to take a certain role. But this is a softer portrait of her. She was an extraordinary woman, a towering figure in 20th-century dance. There were other people around her who realized we needed an English ballet, but she realized that first you needed a school and that from the school and from good teaching would come your ballet company. And she followed that vision through. Her book *Invitation to the Ballet*, which we've used as the title to the exhibition, came out in 1937, and it's like a manifesto: this is the kind of repertory you need, this is the type of training you need, this is how many dancers you need for the repertory, and so on. She acknowledges her influences and her collaborators, but at the same time she is incredibly visionary.

Opposite page: picture reproduced by permission of the Stannus family

This page, bottom: picture reproduced by permission of Germaine Kanova

69

De Valois' own choreographic notes for *Job* (1931, De Valois) and examples of her own design drawings. When she came into the studio to rehearse she came with the floor plan, with her notebook, with her drawings. None of it was worked out in the studios with the dancers – she would know exactly what she wanted. Some of her younger dancers have told us that they would sometimes go to her home where she would make the dinner and then sit down on the floor with her notebook and draw these little stick figures on her choreographic notebook page, working out the choreography for her next ballet. The drawings for *Job* are slightly more polished, very much influenced by Blake's drawings – you can see that in her seated figures. It illustrates how much she was influenced by British sensibilities and by the 18th century, as in *The Rake's Progress* and *The Prospect Before Us*.

ORTERS....cont'd.

4) TURN SLOWLY TO RIGHT (Heaven..up stage)..APPEALING TO HEAVEN.
                     Count 8.

xxxxxxxxxxxxxxxxxxxxxxxxxxxxxxxxxxxxxxxxxxxxxxxxxxxxxxxxxxx

5) VISION OF HELL...immediately.
      KNEEL in same position as above but bow the head.

xxxxxxxxxxxxxxxxxxxxxxxxxxxxxxxxxxxxxxxxxxxxxxxxxxxxxxxxxxx

6) AS SATAN SITS ON THRONE.....TURN and KNEEL on BOTH KNEES.
      Right knee slightly forward..right hip forward...
      Arms down...bend to left..Head up and Right.
      CADENZA..and HOLD for 9 counts.

xxxxxxxxxxxxxxxxxxxxxxxxxxxxxxxxxxxxxxxxxxxxxxxxxxxxxxxxxxx

7) Rise slowly and SIT(to count of 6.)..HOLD FOR COUNTS OF
                          3 & 6.

xxxxxxxxxxxxxxxxxxxxxxxxxxxxxxxxxxxxxxxxxxxxxxxxxxxxxxxxxxx

8) Change to position below and ROLL BODY ROUND...to a
              COUNT of 6.

xxxxxxxxxxxxxxxxxxxxxxxxxxxxxxxxxxxxxxxxxxxxxxxxxxxxxxxxxxx

psis of counts from CADENZA: SEGUE INTO:
          9....NIL.
          6....JOB RISES.
          3....Mrs.JOB.
          6....COMFORTERS.
          6....JOB ROLLS.
          6....Mrs.JOB ROLLS.

The costume worn by Margot Fonteyn as the Lady Dulcinea in *Don Quixote* (1950, De Valois) with a newspaper photograph (above) of her performing in the costume with Robert Helpmann. *Don Quixote* was a one-act narrative ballet and received very mixed reviews. People came expecting a comic ballet, very much in the way that *The Prospect Before Us* before it was a comic ballet and with Helpmann playing the type of clown role she created for him in that ballet. But this was a darker take on the Don Quixote story and the audience didn't quite know how to respond. Her designer was Edward Burra, and we are fortunate to have the costume he designed for Fonteyn as the Lady Dulcinea. She plays a vision-like figure similar to other roles she created, but she also played the earthy innkeeper's wife Aldonza and is said to have particularly enjoyed the contrast between the roles. De Valois was very busy at the time: companies at Covent Garden and Sadler's Wells (the touring wing of the ballet) and the School. Sadly, she seems to have decided that she didn't have enough time for choreography, so this is the last work she created for The Royal Ballet.

Talking to dancers (*Agon*, 1957, MacMillan). Above left: De Valois with Kenneth MacMillan in a break in the rehearsal (you can also see the back of the designer Nicholas Georgiadis). De Valois very much encouraged MacMillan to try choreography. He was by all accounts a wonderful dancer – whether in such *danseur noble* roles as Florestan in *The Sleeping Beauty* or in the great character parts in such ballets as *The Lady and the Fool*, in which he played a clown figure. But he suffered terribly from stage fright, so De Valois encouraged him to choreograph. He'd begun choreographing for the sister company's choreographic workshops and De Valois had immediately seen that he was someone with a serious talent. So, quite soon after, she commissioned him to create *Danses concertantes*.

Middle: Demonstrating hand movements (*Job*, 1931, De Valois). This photograph is from 1948, the first time that *Job* was performed at the Royal Opera House. Here she is demonstrating to the dancers. She had this very fixed idea in her mind of what she wanted and would sometimes go over exactly the same point in the same way with different generations of dancers.

Above right: Completing the make-up for a dancer with Sadler's Wells Opera Ballet (*Khadra*, 1946, Franca). *Khadra* was created for the Sadler's Wells Opera Ballet by Celia Franca. A few years later when someone asked De Valois who might go and start a Canadian ballet company, she suggested Franca. De Valois never saw the Company as being about her choreography, but always had an eye on the future – looking for young choreographers she could encourage. And here she is making up Sheila O'Reilly, who created the role of Khadra – Director of these companies maybe, yet there she is in the wings making sure the make-up is correct. No detail was too small!

Below: Rehearsing in 1950 for a gala to celebrate 25 years of Sadler's Wells Ballet (*A Wedding Bouquet*, Ashton). For some reason the Company celebrated its 25th anniversary in 1950 – it was a year early, but nobody seemed to mind at the time. For it, De Valois revived *A Wedding Bouquet*, which had been created by Ashton in 1937. In one photograph (left) De Valois is teaching the role of Webster, the bossy parlour maid created for her to play as a little bit of a joke – she was big enough to see the joke and was very funny in the role. Right: De Valois is carried off by some of the dancers, with tweed suit and shoes – she obviously didn't have time to get changed for rehearsal, but has just popped in, done her little bit, and would then be off to another meeting.

The Grand defilé at the Gala held in 1964 to mark De Valois' retirement as Director of The Royal Ballet the previous year. She retired in 1963 at the age of 65 and was quite unsentimental about it: the time had come, she handed over to Frederick Ashton and concentrated her energies on the Ballet School and working with the Turkish Ballet (which she founded). Typically she wanted to go with no fuss at all, so nothing could be organized in the actual year she retired. But the following year, Ashton was determined they should have a gala to mark her retirement and pay tribute to her. He organized it and included this Grand defilé: the wonderful thing is that absolutely everybody was in it — the School, the dancers from both companies, her ballet staff. It was a very special moment in the history of the companies and of the School. After, she continued to work and teach at the School, and she certainly advised such people as Ashton and MacMillan, and was still very much a presence and an inspiration to the Company. Her ballets continued to be revived and she would work on passing them on to subsequent generations.

73

A Company Chronology

1930s

1931 20 January Bizet's opera *Carmen* is staged at the newly reopened Sadler's Wells Theatre. The dancers in it come from a fledgling ballet company, the Vic-Wells Opera Ballet, under the creative direction of their founder Ninette de Valois. The result of many developments of this Company – always under De Valois' leadership – would eventually be The Royal Ballet. **5 May** The Company gives its own performance of short works by De Valois at Lilian Baylis's Old Vic theatre. It is Baylis's use of dancers in her operas and plays that gives De Valois the chance to bring her Company together. **July** The Camargo Society presents the Company in a programme which includes De Valois' *Job* and two works by Frederick Ashton, a young dancer also beginning to make his mark as a choreographer.

1932 January Alicia Markova becomes a regular Guest Artist alongside Anton Dolin. **March** *Les Sylphides* is revived with Markova and Dolin. **September** The Company tours for the first time together, to Denmark. **October** Act II of *Le Lac des cygnes* marks the Company's first foray into the classical repertory.

1933 March Nicholas Sergeyev presents the full-length *Coppélia* with Lydia Lopokova as Swanilda. He had been the *régisseur general* of the Mariinsky Theatre, but fled Russia after the October Revolution bringing the written notation necessary to stage many classic Russian ballets.

1934 January Sergeyev puts on *Giselle* with Markova and Dolin. **April** *Casse-Noisette* is presented, again by Sergeyev. **20 November** The full *Le Lac des cygnes* is presented with Markova and Robert Helpmann, who had recently been promoted to Principal with the Company.

1935 Ashton is signed up as a performer and resident choreographer. **20 May** De Valois' *The Rake's Progress* has its first performance, with Markova as the Betrayed Girl. **26 November** Ashton's *Le Baiser de la fée* receives its premiere, with the young Margot Fonteyn in the cast.

1937 The Company represents British culture at the International Exhibition in Paris. **16 February** The premiere of Ashton's *Les Patineurs*. **27 April** A further Ashton premiere with *A Wedding Bouquet*.

5 October De Valois' *Checkmate* receives its first performance in London. **25 November** Lilian Baylis dies.

1939 2 February Sergeyev puts on *The Sleeping Princess* with Fonteyn and Helpmann in the lead roles. **1 September** Germany invades Poland; in response, Britain, France, Australia and New Zealand declare war on Germany.

1940s

1940 23 January The first performance of Ashton's *Dante Sonata*. **May** The Company travels to the Netherlands for a small tour, but the advancing German army forces a hurried escape. **November** The Company begins to tour throughout wartime Britain.

1941 The New Theatre, St Martin's Lane, becomes the Company's home for much of the war, and *The Sleeping Princess* is again staged.

1942 19 May The first performance of Helpmann's ballet *Hamlet*, with Helpmann in the title role.

74

1944 26 October Helpmann's *Miracle in the Gorbals* receives its premiere.

1945 The Company undertakes a tour of the Continent with the Entertainments National Service Association (ENSA), a forces organization. **May 8th** The war ends in Europe.

1946 20 February The Company becomes resident at Covent Garden, and re-opens the Royal Opera House with *The Sleeping Beauty*. **24 April** Ashton's *Symphonic Variations* is performed for the first time.

1947 February De Valois invites Léonide Massine, one of the biggest stars of Diaghilev's Ballets Russes, to revive *The Three-Cornered Hat* and *La Boutique fantasque*.

1948 23 December Ashton's *Cinderella* receives its premiere: it is the Company's first home-grown full-length ballet.

1949 9 October The Company presents *The Sleeping Beauty* in New York, the start of a hugely successful tour that takes in many cities in the USA and Canada.

1950s

1950 20 February The first performance of De Valois' *Don Quixote*. **5 April** George Balanchine and his New York City Ballet make their first European visit, Balanchine reviving his *Ballet Imperial* for Sadler's Wells Ballet. **5 May** Roland Petit's creation for the Company, *Ballabile,* receives its premiere. **September** The Company embarks on a five-month, 32-city tour of the USA.

1951 21 August Music Director Constant Lambert, one of the chief architects of the Company with De Valois and Ashton, dies aged 45.

1952 3 September The first performance of Ashton's *Sylvia*.

1953 2 June Coronation gala for HM The Queen, which includes a specially devised ballet by Ashton for the occasion, *Homage to the Queen*.

1954 23 August For the 25th anniversary of Diaghilev's death, the Company joins the Edinburgh Festival tributes with a performance of *The Firebird*; Fonteyn dances the title role.

1956 1 March Kenneth MacMillan creates his first ballet for the Sadler's Wells Ballet, *Noctambules*. **31 October** The Sadler's Wells Ballet, the Sadler's Wells Theatre Ballet and the School are granted a Royal Charter – the main Company becoming The Royal Ballet.

1957 1 January John Cranko's *The Prince of the Pagodas*, to a score by Benjamin Britten, is given its first performance at Covent Garden. It is the first full-length work to a modern commissioned score to be presented in the West.

1958 27 October Ashton's new ballet *Ondine*, created for Fonteyn, opens with her in the title role; the new score is by Hans Werner Henze.

1959 13 March MacMillan's *Danses concertantes*, created for Sadler's Wells Theatre Ballet in 1955, opens at Covent Garden.

Below: Violetta Elvin as Sylvia, John Field as Aminta, Alexander Grant as Eros, and members of the Sadler's Wells Ballet in Ashton's *Sylvia* (1952)

Photograph: Roger Wood / © Royal Opera House Collections

1960s

1960 28 January The premiere of Ashton's 'tribute to nature', *La Fille mal gardée* with Nadia Nerina dancing the role of Lise to David Blair's Colas.

1961 15 June The Company makes its first tour of Russia presenting *Ondine* on the first night; an exchange agreement sees the Kirov Ballet perform at Covent Garden.

1962 21 February Rudolf Nureyev, having controversially defected from the Bolshoi in 1961, makes his debut as Albrecht to Fonteyn's Giselle. **3 May** MacMillan's new version of *The Rite of Spring*, with Monica Mason as the Chosen Maiden, is given its first performance.

1963 12 March Ashton's *Marguerite and Armand*, created for Fonteyn and Nureyev, opens. **7 May** De Valois retires as Director of the Company and Ashton succeeds her, while De Valois becomes supervisor of The Royal Ballet School. **28 November** Nureyev's first staging for The Royal Ballet is the 'Kingdom of the Shades' scene from *La Bayadère*.

1964 29 February Antoinette Sibley dances Aurora in the Company's 400th performance of *The Sleeping Beauty*. **2 April** The Company's contributions to the celebrations of the 400th anniversary of Shakespeare's birth include Ashton's *The Dream*, which launches the dance partnership of Sibley and Anthony Dowell. **2 December** Bronislava Nijinska, younger sister of Nijinsky, revives her *Les Biches*, with Svetlana Beriosova as the Hostess.

1965 9 February MacMillan's first full-length work, *Romeo and Juliet*, is presented; created for Lynn Seymour and Christopher Gable, the opening night is danced by Fonteyn and Nureyev.

1966 23 March Nijinska revives her *Les Noces* in a double bill with *Les Biches*. **May** MacMillan takes up the ballet directorship of the Deutsche Oper Berlin. **19 May** MacMillan's *Song of the Earth*, created for Cranko's Stuttgart Ballet, is given its Covent Garden premiere.

1967 25 January Antony Tudor creates his first work for The Royal Ballet, *Shadowplay*.

1968 29 February The premiere of Nureyev's version of *The Nutcracker*. **26 April** The Company makes the official announcement of Ashton's retirement as Director in 1970 and his succession by MacMillan. **25 October** The premiere of Ashton's *Enigma Variations*. **12 November** Tudor revives his 1938 production of *Lilac Garden*.

1970s

1971 22 July MacMillan's long-awaited *Anastasia* opens, with Seymour in the lead role. **4 August** The premiere of American choreographer Glen Tetley's contemporary ballet *Field Figures*.

1972 20 June Natalia Makarova dances Giselle, partnered by Dowell, making her debut at Covent Garden as a Guest Artist.

1973 8 June At Covent Garden, Nureyev and Makarova dance *The Sleeping Beauty* together for the first time.

1974 7 March Sibley, Dowell and David Wall dance the opening night of MacMillan's *Manon*. **7 October** The premiere of MacMillan's *Elite Syncopations* with Wayne Sleep in the Principal Character role.

1987 12 March *Swan Lake*, with Cynthia Harvey and Jonathan Cope, is Dowell's first production as Director. **16 December** Ashton stages a revival of *Cinderella*, his final production for The Royal Ballet.

1988 9 March Bintley's *'Still Life' at the Penguin Café* receives its world premiere with the Company. **19 August** Ashton dies in the year in which his *Ondine* is revived by Dowell after an absence of 22 years from the repertory.

1989 18 May The full-length *La Bayadère* is first given by The Royal Ballet in a new production by Makarova. **8 December** MacMillan's final, full-evening production, *The Prince of the Pagodas*, is created for the Company, with Darcey Bussell and Jonathan Cope.

Left: Lynn Seymour and Anthony Dowell in Ashton's *A Month in the Country* (1976)

Photograph: Leslie E. Spatt

Below: Philip Broomhead as Southern Cape Zebra in Bintley's *'Still Life' at the Penguin Café* (1988)

Photograph: Leslie E. Spatt

1975 April The Royal Ballet makes its first tour of the Far East.

1976 12 February The first performance of Ashton's *A Month in the Country*, with Dowell and Seymour.

1977 13 June Norman Morrice succeeds MacMillan as Director of The Royal Ballet.

1978 14 February The premiere of MacMillan's full-length ballet *Mayerling*, the Principal male role created for David Wall.

1980s

1980 13 March MacMillan's *Gloria* receives its premiere.
4 August Ashton creates *Rhapsody* for Lesley Collier and Mikhail Baryshnikov, given at a performance for the 80th birthday of HM Queen Elizabeth The Queen Mother.

1981 30 April World premiere of MacMillan's *Isadora* with Merle Park in the title role, to celebrate the Company's golden jubilee.

1982 2 December The premiere of Nureyev's *The Tempest*.

1984 24 February MacMillan's *Different Drummer* is created for the Company. **20 December** Collier and Dowell perform in the first night of Peter Wright's Biedermeier-inspired production of *The Nutcracker*.

1986 Anthony Dowell is appointed Director of The Royal Ballet.

77

1990s

1990 19 July MacMillan's 'Farewell' *pas de deux* with Bussell and Irek Mukhamedov is performed at a London Palladium gala.

1991 7 February The first night of MacMillan's *Winter Dreams* (which grew out of the *'Farewell' pas de deux*) . **2 May** In celebration of the 60th anniversary of the Company, Bintley's *Cyrano* is first performed at a Royal Gala.

1992 13 February William Forsythe's *In the middle, somewhat elevated* is first performed by the Company. **19 March** MacMillan's last work, *The Judas Tree*, created for Mukhamedov and Viviana Durante, receives its premiere. **29 October** MacMillan dies of a heart attack at the first performance of a major revival of his *Mayerling*. **6 December** Ashton's *Tales of Beatrix Potter* is first staged live by The Royal Ballet.

1993 7 April Baryshnikov's *Don Quixote* is first performed by the Company in new designs.

1994 6 April A new production of *The Sleeping Beauty* by Anthony Dowell is performed in Washington in the presence of the President of the USA and HRH The Princess Margaret. **18 June** Ashley Page's *Fearful Symmetries* is first performed (receiving the 1995 Olivier Award for Best New Dance Production). **3 November** Dowell's production of *The Sleeping Beauty* with designs by Maria Björnson is first performed at the Royal Opera House for a Royal Gala.

1996 2 May MacMillan's *Anastasia* is performed with new sets and costumes by Bob Crowley.

1997 14 July Farewell Gala and final performance at the 'old' Royal Opera House. During the closure The Royal Ballet is 'on tour', performing at Labatt's Apollo, Hammersmith, the Royal Festival Hall and the Barbican.

1999 December The redeveloped Royal Opera House opens. The Royal Ballet's first programme is 'A Celebration of International Choreography' **17 December** The opening night of *The Nutcracker* is the first performance of a full-length ballet in the new House.

2000s

2000 8 February Revival of De Valois' production of *Coppélia* in the original designs by Osbert Lancaster opens. **29 February** Ashton's *Marguerite and Armand* is revived with Sylvie Guillem and Nicolas Le Riche in the title roles. **6 May** Millicent Hodson and Kenneth Archer produce a major restaging of Nijinsky's *Jeux* in a programme with *L'Après-midi d'un faune*.

2001 8 March De Valois dies. **July** Dowell retires as Director of The Royal Ballet. **23 October** The first performance of Nureyev's version of *Don Quixote* by The Royal Ballet, which marks the first performance under Ross Stretton's tenure as Director. **22 November** The first performance by The Royal Ballet of Cranko's *Onegin*.

2002 9 February HRH The Princess Margaret, Countess of Snowdon, President of The Royal Ballet, dies. **September** Ross Stretton resigns as Director. **December** Monica Mason becomes Director of the Company.

2003 13 January The Company dances Jiří Kylián's *Sinfonietta* for the first time. **8 March** The premiere of Makarova's new production of *The Sleeping Beauty*. **22 December** Wendy Ellis Somes's new production of *Cinderella* receives its premiere.

2004 April The Royal Ballet pays homage to Serge Diaghilev in a 75th anniversary tribute programme that includes the Company premiere of *Le Spectre de la rose*. **4 November** The premiere of Ashton's full-length *Sylvia*, reconstructed and staged by Christopher Newton for the 'Ashton 100' celebrations.

2005 7 May The premiere of a new work by Christopher Bruce, inspired by the life of Jimi Hendrix: *Three Songs – Two Voices*.

2006 15 May The Company begins its 75th anniversary celebrations with a new production of the 1946 *Sleeping Beauty*, realized by Monica Mason and Christopher Newton with Messel's original designs, re-created by Peter Farmer, followed by revivals of Ashton's *Homage to The Queen*, with additional new choreography by Christopher Wheeldon, Michael Corder and David Bintley, and De Valois' *The Rake's Progress*. **8 June** A gala performance of *Homage* preceded by *La Valse* and *divertissements* is attended by HM The Queen. **November** The premieres of Wayne McGregor's *Chroma* and Wheeldon's *DGV: Danse à grande vitesse*. **December** McGregor becomes Resident Choreographer of The Royal Ballet.

2007 March Alastair Marriott's *Children of Adam* receives its premiere. **April** Will Tuckett's *The Seven Deadly Sins* receives its premiere. **June** Barry Wordsworth is appointed Music Director. **8 June** Darcey Bussell retires as a Principal. **23 November** The Royal Ballet performs Balanchine's *Jewels* in its entirety for the first time.

2008 28 February The first performance of Wheeldon's *Electric Counterpoint*. **23 April** The mainstage choreographic debut of Kim Brandstrup with *Rushes: Fragments of a Lost Story*. **15 June to 21 July** The Royal Ballet goes on tour in China and the Far East, performing in Beijing, Shanghai, Tokyo, Osaka and Hong Kong. **October** marks the 50th anniversary of Ashton's *Ondine*. **13 November** The premiere of McGregor's *Infra*.

2009 March Anthony Russell Roberts retires as Artistic Administrator and is succeeded by Kevin O'Hare. **April** Jeanetta Laurence is appointed Associate Director of The Royal Ballet. **June–July** The Royal Ballet tours to Washington D.C., Granada and Havana. **4 November** Wayne McGregor's *Limen* receives its premiere in a mixed programme with Glen Tetley's *Sphinx*, which enters the repertory for the first time. **17 November** A service to dedicate a memorial to the founders of The Royal Ballet is held at Westminster Abbey.

2010s

2010 50th anniversary of Ashton's *La Fille mal gardée*. **19 February** Mainstage choreographic debut of Royal Ballet First Artist Jonathan Watkins with *As One*. **23 April** Miyako Yoshida dances her last performance with the Company at the Royal Opera House as Cinderella. **5 May** Mainstage choreographic debut of Royal Ballet First Artist Liam Scarlett with *Asphodel Meadows*. **June–July** The Royal Ballet tours to Japan for the tenth time (Tokyo and Osaka) and Spain (Barcelona). **29 June** Miyako Yoshida retires from the Company, dancing her last Juliet in Toyko.

Below: Tamara Rojo and Steven McRae in McGregor's *Chroma* (2006)

Photograph: Johan Persson

79

HAROLD TURNER

An important figure in early British ballet, Harold Turner was an exceptional virtuoso dancer not only for his time but also setting the standard for future generations of male dancers. His energetic and athletic technique inspired Ashton to create on him the Blue Boy in *Les Patineurs*, which was arguably his greatest role. He was also widely praised as the first Red Knight in De Valois' *Checkmate*, and danced all the great, classical roles of the time including Frantz, Albrecht and Blue Bird, as well as performing in such works inherited from Ballet Russes as *Les Sylphides* and *Carnaval*.

Born in 1909, Turner trained in Manchester with Alfred Haines and danced in his company. His outstanding talent was widely noticed and in 1929 he moved to London, appearing in various, new British companies including Dolin's, Karsavina's and Rambert's. He danced in many of Ashton's early works and created roles in *Nymphs and Shepherds* and *Capriol Suite*, as well as in De Valois' *Suite of Dances* and *Cephalus and Procris*. In 1935, Turner joined Vic-Wells Ballet and became one of its most popular dancers, creating roles in De Valois' *The Rake's Progress*, *Checkmate*, *The Emperor's New Clothes* and *Don Quixote*, and in Ashton's *Le Baiser de la fée*, *Apparitions*, *A Wedding Bouquet* and *Les Patineurs*.

During World War II, Turner danced in other companies and also served in the RAF. As he grew older, he took on character roles including the Rake in *The Rake's Progress* and the Miller in Massine's *The Three-Cornered Hat*. After retiring, he worked as a teacher at Sadler's Wells School and Ballet Master at the Covent Garden Opera Ballet. He was preparing to return to the stage for Massine's *The Good Humoured Ladies* in 1962 when he died during rehearsals at the Royal Opera House. Turner and Royal Ballet dancer, teacher and répétiteur Gerd Larsen, were married in 1944 and are survived by their daughter, Solveig.

ALEXANDER GRANT

One of the 20th century's greatest character dancers, Alexander Grant has become best known for the roles he created for Ashton including Eros in *Sylvia* (where he impersonated a statue and was required to stand still for almost the entire first act), the Jester in *Cinderella*, Tirrenio in *Ondine*, Alain in *La Fille mal gardée*, Bottom in *The Dream*, as well as roles in *Daphnis and Chloé*, *Birthday Offering*, *Persephone*, *Jazz Calendar*, *Enigma Variations* and *A Month in the Country*.

Born in New Zealand, Grant trained with Kathleen O'Brien and Jean Horne before winning a Royal Academy of Dancing scholarship. However, World War II meant he had to postpone studying in London and instead he performed as a singer and dancer for troops in the Pacific. When he did join the Sadler's Wells Ballet, he gained wide recognition for his role as the Barber in Massine's 1947 revival of *Mam'zelle Angot*. Two years later, Grant was made Soloist. He became The Royal Ballet's leading character

artist, creating many roles for them; and he also created the role of Drosselmeyer for the Joffrey Ballet's 1987 production of *The Nutcracker*. In the early 1970s, Grant ran The Royal Ballet's educational group, Ballet for All, but in 1976 he left the Company to become Artistic Director of the National Ballet of Canada, a post he held until 1983, and in the mid-to-late 1980s, he danced and coached at London Festival Ballet. Now the custodian of Ashton's *La Fille mal gardée*, he currently rehearses productions of the ballet for companies across the world.

LESLEY COLLIER

Lesley Collier became one of the most popular Royal Ballet dancers during a dancing career that spanned three decades with the Company. An incredibly versatile dancer with a unique combination of virtuosity and musicality, she performed all the classical ballerina roles as well as the dramatic heroines in MacMillan's repertory and the comic heroine in Ashton's *La Fille mal gardée*. In 1980, for The Queen Mother's 80th birthday performance, she famously danced with Baryshnikov in Ashton's *Rhapsody*, her role in it created by him to display her fast footwork and expressive upper body.

Born in Orpington, Collier won a scholarship to The Royal Ballet School and took private lessons from Winifred Edwards. She joined the Company in 1965 and was promoted to Soloist in 1970

and Principal in 1972. Besides *Rhapsody*, Collier also created roles in MacMillan's *Elite Syncopations* and *Four Seasons*, Tetley's *Dances of Albion*, Van Manen's *Four Schumann Pieces*, Nureyev's *The Tempest* and Bintley's *Consort Lessons*, *Galantries* and *Cyrano*.

Her television appearances included *The Dancing Princesses* and *Dizzy Feet*. Collier was a guest star at the World Ballet Festival, Tokyo, 1982. She received the 1987 *Evening Standard* Ballet Award and was made a CBE in 1993. In 1995 she retired from dancing and became Ballet Mistress at The Royal Ballet School. Since 2000, Collier has been coaching Soloists and Principals in the Company.

Left: Alexander Grant as Alain with Lesley Edwards as Thomas in Ashton's *La Fille mal gardée* (1960)
Photograph: © Houston Rogers/V&A Images/V&A Theatre Collections
Below: Lesley Collier and Mikhail Baryshnikov in Ashton's *Rhapsody* (1980)
Photograph: Nobby Clark/Arena Pal

Artistic and Administrative Staff

Artistic Staff

Back Row *Left to right,* Grant Coyle, Philip Mosley, Clare Thurman, Wayne McGregor, Christopher Saunders, David Pickering, Gary Avis, Anna Trevien.
Front Row *(seated), Left to right,* Elizabeth Anderton, Lesley Collier, Jeanetta Laurence, Ursula Hageli, Sian Murphy. Staff also includes: Christopher Carr, Alexander Agadzhanov, Jonathan Cope and Mayumi Hotta.
Photograph: Rob Moore

Administration
Standing *Left to right,* Heather Baxter, Andrew Hurst, Kitty Greenleaf, Gavin Fitzpatrick, Orsola Ricciardelli, Rosie Neave, Yvonne Hunte, Kevin O'Hare.
Seated *Left to right,* Elizabeth Ferguson and Hayley Starling.
Photograph: Rob Moore

82

Music Staff, Physiotherapy and Body Control Instructors, and Stage Management

Music Staff
Standing (left to right)
Jonathan Beavis,
Paul Stobart, Barry
Wordsworth; *Seated* (left
to right) Philip Cornfield,
Richard Coates, Kate
Shipway, Robert Clark
Photograph: Rob Moore

Stage Management
Left to right, Lucy
Summers, Lynne Otto,
Johanna Adams Farley
Photograph: Rob Moore

**Physiotherapy
and Body Control
Instructors**
Left to right, Moira
McCormack, Daryl
Martin, Fiona Kleckham,
Jane Paris. Staff
also includes: Helen
Wellington, Konrad
Simpson, Britt Tajet-
Foxell, Tatina Semprini.
Photograph: Rob Moore

Principal Guest Artists and Principals

**PRINCIPAL
GUEST ARTISTS**

Carlos Acosta
Joined as Principal 1998, Principal
Guest Artist 2003
Born: Havana, Cuba
Trained: National Ballet School
of Cuba
Previous Companies: English National
Ballet (1991), National Ballet of Cuba
(1992), Houston Ballet (1993)

PRINCIPALS

Leanne Benjamin
Joined 1992
Promoted to Principal 1993
Born: Rockhampton, Australia
Trained: The Royal Ballet School

Federico Bonelli
Joined as Principal 2003
Born: Genoa, Italy
Trained: Turin Dance Academy
Previous Companies: Zurich Ballet
(1996), Dutch National Ballet (1999)

Alina Cojocaru
Joined 1999
Promoted to Principal 2001
Born: Bucharest, Romania
Trained: Kiev Ballet School,
The Royal Ballet School
Previous Company: Kiev Ballet
(1998)

Lauren Cuthbertson
Joined 2002
Promoted to Principal 2008
Born: Devon, England
Trained: The Royal Ballet School

Mara Galeazzi
Joined 1992
Promoted to Principal 2003
Born: Brescia, Italy
Trained: La Scala Ballet School,
Milan

Nehemiah Kish
Joined as Principal 2010
Born: Michigan, USA
Trained: National Ballet School of
Canada
Previous Company: Royal Danish
Ballet

Johan Kobborg
Joined as Principal 1999
Born: Odense, Denmark
Trained: Royal Danish Ballet School
Previous Company: Royal Danish
Ballet (1991)

Sarah Lamb
Joined 2004
Promoted to Principal 2006
Born: Boston, USA
Trained: Boston Ballet School
Previous Company: Boston Ballet
(1998)

84

David Makhateli
Joined 2003
Promoted to Principal 2008
Born: Tbilisi, Georgia
Trained: The Royal Ballet School

Roberta Marquez
Joined and promoted to Principal
2004
Born: Rio de Janeiro, Brazil
Trained: Maria Olenewa State Dance
School
Previous Company: Municipal
Theatre Ballet, Rio de Janeiro (1994)

Steven McRae
Joined 2004
Promoted to Principal 2009
Born: Sydney, Australia
Trained: The Royal Ballet School

Laura Morera
Joined 1995
Promoted to Principal 2007
Born: Madrid, Spain
Trained: The Royal Ballet School

Marianela Nuñez
Joined 1998
Promoted to Principal 2002
Born: Buenos Aires
Trained: Teatro Colón Ballet School,
The Royal Ballet School

Rupert Pennefather
Joined 1999
Promoted to Principal 2008
Born: Maidenhead, England
Trained: The Royal Ballet School

Sergei Polunin
Joined 2007
Promoted to Principal 2010
Born: Ukraine
Trained: The Royal Ballet School

Tamara Rojo
Joined as Principal 1999
Born: Montreal, Canada
Trained: Victor Ullate Ballet School,
Madrid
Previous Companies: Victor Ullate
Ballet (1991), Scottish Ballet (1996),
English National Ballet (1997)

Thiago Soares
Joined 2002
Promoted to Principal 2006
Born: São Gonçalo, Brazil
Trained: Centre for Dance, Rio de
Janeiro
Previous Company: Rio de Janeiro
Municipal Theatre Ballet (1998)

Edward Watson
Joined 1994
Promoted to Principal 2005
Born: Bromley, England
Trained: The Royal Ballet School

Zenaida Yanowsky
Joined 1994
Promoted to Principal 2001
Born: Lyon, France
Trained: Las Palmas, Majorca
Previous Company: Paris Opéra
Ballet (1994)

**PRINCIPAL
CHARACTER ARTISTS**
Left to right
**Gary Avis
Alastair Marriott
Elizabeth McGorian
Genesia Rosato**

Christopher Saunders

**CHARACTER ARTIST
Philip Mosley**

FIRST SOLOISTS
Left to right
**Ricardo Cervera
Deirdre Chapman**

**Yuhui Choe
Helen Crawford
Bennet Gartside
Valeri Hristov**

**Hikaru Kobayashi
José Martín
Itziar Mendizabal
Johannes Stepanek**

Company Members 2010/11

SOLOISTS
Left to right
Christina Arestis
Melissa Hamilton
Victoria Hewitt
Ryoichi Hirano

Jonathan Howells
Paul Kay
Bethany Keating
Kenta Kura

Iohna Loots
Brian Maloney
Laura McCulloch
Kristen McNally

David Pickering
Samantha Raine
Eric Underwood
Thomas Whitehead

First Artists and Artists

Company Members 2010/11

FIRST ARTISTS
Left to right
Tara-Brigitte Bhavnani
Claire Calvert
Leanne Cope
Olivia Cowley

Vanessa Fenton
Francesca Filpi
Nathalie Harrison
Elizabeth Harrod

Emma Maguire
Pietra Mello-Pittman
Fernando Montaño
Erico Montes

Sian Murphy
Ludovic Ondiviela
Romany Pajdak
Liam Scarlett

**Michael Stojko
Akane Takada
Lara Turk
Andrej Uspenski**

**Jonathan Watkins
James Wilkie**

ARTISTS
Left to right
**Ruth Bailey
Sander Blommaert
Camille Bracher
James Butcher**

**Jacqueline Clark
Celisa Diuana
Tristan Dyer
Benjamin Ella**

Artists

Kevin Emerton
Hayley Forskitt
Elsa Godard
James Hay

Yasmine Naghdi
Demelza Parish
Gemma Pitchley-Gale
Beatriz Stix-Brunell

Leticia Stock
Dawid Trzensimiech
Sabina Westcombe
Valentino Zucchetti

90

The Royal Ballet 2010/11

Director Dame Monica Mason DBE
Associate Director Jeanetta Laurence
Administrative Director Kevin O'Hare

Music Director Barry Wordsworth
Resident Choreographer
Wayne McGregor

Company Manager
Andrew Hurst

Financial Controller
Heather Baxter

**Artistic Administrator
and Character Artist**
Philip Mosley

**Acting Contracts
Administrator**
Sarah Meniker

**Deputy Company
Manager**
Elizabeth Ferguson

**Administrative
Co-ordinator**
Yvonne Hunte

**Management
Accountant**
Orsola Ricciardelli

**Artistic Administrative
Assistant**
Gavin Fitzpatrick

Education Manager
Clare Thurman

**Artistic and Education
Co-ordinator**
David Pickering

**Head of Physiotherapy
and Chartered
Physiotherapist**
Moira McCormack

**Chartered
Physiotherapists**
Daryl Martin
Aedin Kennedy

**Body Control
Instructors**
Jane Paris
Fiona Kleckham

**Occupational
Psychologist**
Britt Tajet-Foxell

Masseurs
Fatina Semprini
Konrad Simpson
Helen Wellington

**Consultant Orthopaedic
Surgeon**
Lloyd Williams

Medical Advisor
Ian Beasley

Ballet Masters
Christopher Saunders
Gary Avis

Ballet Mistress
Ursula Hageli

Assistant Ballet Mistress
Sian Murphy

**Senior Teacher and
Répétiteur to the
Principal Artists**
Alexander Agadzhanov

Répétiteurs
Lesley Collier
Jonathan Cope

**Principal Dance Notator
and Répétiteur**
Grant Coyle

Dance Notators
Mayumi Hotta
Anna Trevien

Head of Music Staff
Robert Clark

Music Staff
Jonathan Beavis
Richard Coates
Philip Cornfield
Kate Shipway
Paul Stobart

**Guest Principal
Ballet Master**
Christopher Carr

Principal Guest Teacher
Elizabeth Anderton

Guest Teachers
Loipa Araujo
Johnny Eliasen
Olga Evreinoff
David Howard
Roland Price

Conductors
Daniel Capps
Boris Gruzin
Koen Kessels
Paul Murphy
Valeriy Ovsyanikov
Pavel Sorokin
Barry Wordsworth
Martin Yates

Principals
Carlos Acosta†
Leanne Benjamin
Federico Bonelli
Alina Cojocaru
Guillaume Côté††
Lauren Cuthbertson
Mara Galeazzi
Nehemiah Kish
Johan Kobborg
Sarah Lamb
David Makhateli
Roberta Marquez
Steven McRae
Laura Morera
Marianela Nuñez
Rupert Pennefather
Sergei Polunin
Tamara Rojo
Thiago Soares
Edward Watson
Zenaida Yanowsky

**Principal Character
Artists**
Gary Avis
David Drew††
Alastair Marriott
Elizabeth McGorian
Genesia Rosato
Christopher Saunders
William Tuckett††

First Soloists
Ricardo Cervera
Deirdre Chapman
Yuhui Choe
Helen Crawford
Bennet Gartside
Valeri Hristov
Hikaru Kobayashi
José Martín
Itziar Mendizabal
Johannes Stepanek

Soloists
Christina Arestis
Melissa Hamilton
Victoria Hewitt
Ryoichi Hirano
Jonathan Howells
Paul Kay
Bethany Keating
Kenta Kura
Iohna Loots
Brian Maloney
Laura McCulloch
Kristen McNally
David Pickering
Samantha Raine
Eric Underwood
Thomas Whitehead

First Artists
Tara-Brigitte Bhavnani
Claire Calvert
Leanne Cope
Olivia Cowley
Vanessa Fenton
Francesca Filpi
Nathalie Harrison
Elizabeth Harrod
Emma Maguire
Pietra Mello-Pittman
Fernando Montaño
Erico Montes
Sian Murphy
Ludovic Ondiviela
Romany Pajdak
Liam Scarlett
Michael Stojko
Akane Takada
Lara Turk
Andrej Uspenski
Jonathan Watkins
James Wilkie

Artists
Ruth Bailey
Sander Blommaert
Camille Bracher
James Butcher
Jacqueline Clark
Celisa Diuana
Tristan Dyer
Benjamin Ella
Kevin Emerton
Hayley Forskitt
Elsa Godard
James Hay
Yasmine Naghdi
Demelza Parish
Gemma Pitchley-Gale
Beatriz Stix-Brunell
Leticia Stock
Dawid Trzensimiech
Sabina Westcombe
Valentino Zucchetti

91

† Principal Guest Artist
††Guest Artist

The Royal Ballet on DVD and Blu-ray

WWW.ROH.ORG.UK/RBSHOP

Three Ballets
by Kenneth MacMillan
The Royal Ballet
Music: Joplin (*Elite Syncopations*),
Elias (*The Judas Tree*),
Shostakovich (*Concerto*)
Choreography: MacMillan
Casts: Lamb, Galeazzi, Hristov,
McRae/Acosta, Benjamin, Watson,
Gartside/Choe, McRae, Nuñez,
Pennefather, Crawford.
Orchestra of the Royal Opera
House/Clark, Wordsworth, Grier.
Recorded 2010. DVD/Blu-ray

The Nutcracker
The Royal Ballet
Music: Tchaikovsky
Choreography: Wright/Ivanov
Cast: Yoshida, McRae, Avis, Loots,
Cervera
Orchestra of the Royal Opera
House/Kessels
Recorded 2010
DVD/Blu-ray

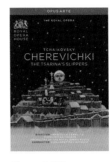

Cherevichki
(The Tsarina's Slippers)
The Royal Opera with Dancers of
The Royal Ballet
Music: Tchaikovsky
Choreography: Alastair Marriott
Cast: Galeazzi, Avis
Orchestra of the Royal Opera
House/Polianichko
Recorded 2010
DVD/Blu-ray

Swan Lake
The Royal Ballet
Music: Tchaikovsky
Choreography: Petipa and Ivanov
Cast: Nuñez, Soares, McGorian,
Saunders, Marriott, Pickering,
Artists of The Royal Ballet
Orchestra of the Royal Opera House/
Ovsyanikov
Recorded 2009
DVD Opus Arte OA1015D
All regions (NTSC)
Blu-ray Opus Arte OABD7042D

Mayerling
The Royal Ballet
Music: Liszt (arr. Lanchbery)
Choreography: MacMillan
Cast: Watson, Galeazzi, Lamb,
Artists of The Royal Ballet
Orchestra of the Royal Opera
House/Wordsworth
Recorded 2009
DVD (Opus Arte OA1028D)
All regions (NTSC)
Blu-ray (Opus Arte OABD7061D)

Ondine
The Royal Ballet
Music: Henze
Choreography: Ashton
Cast: Yoshida, Watson,
Rosato, Cervera, Avis, Artists
of The Royal Ballet
Orchestra of the Royal Opera
House/Wordsworth
Recorded 2010
DVD (Opus Arte OA1030D)
All regions (NTSC)
Blu-ray (Opus Arte OABD7064D)

Dido and Aeneas
The Royal Opera/The Royal Ballet
Music: Purcell
Choreography: McGregor
Cast: Connolly, Meacham, Crowe,
Fulgoni, dancers of The Royal Ballet
Orchestra of the Age of
Enlightenment/Hogwood
Recorded 2009
DVD (Opus Arte OA1018D)
All regions (NTSC)
Blu-ray (Opus Arte OABD7049D)

Acis and Galatea
The Royal Opera/The Royal Ballet
Music: Handel
Choreography: McGregor
Cast: De Niese, Cuthbertson,
Workman, Watson, Agnew, McRae,
Rose, Underwood, Park, Paul Kay,
dancers of The Royal Ballet
Orchestra of the Age of
Enlightenment/Hogwood
Royal Opera Extra Chorus
Recorded 2009
DVD (Opus Arte OA1025D)
All regions (NTSC)
Blu-ray (Opus Arte OABD7056D)

Manon

The Royal Ballet
Music: Massenet
Choreography: MacMillan
Cast: Rojo, Acosta, Martín,
Saunders, Morera, Artists of The
Royal Ballet
Orchestra of the Royal Opera
House/Yates
Recorded 2008
DVD (DECCA 0743346)
All regions (NTSC)

Romeo and Juliet

The Royal Ballet
Music: Prokofiev
Choreography: MacMillan
Cast: Rojo, Acosta, Martin, Soares,
Conley, Saunders, McGorian,
Pickering, Sasaki
and Artists of The Royal Ballet
Royal Ballet Sinfonia/Gruzin
Recorded 2007
DECCA 0743347
All regions (NTSC)
DECCA 0743336BR

The Sleeping Beauty

Music: Tchaikovsky
Choreography: Petipa, Ashton,
Dowell, Wheeldon
Cast: Cojocaru, Bonelli,
Saunders, McGorian,
Marriott, Rosato, Nuñez
Orchestra of the Royal Opera
House/Ovsyanikov
Recorded 2007
BBC Opus Arte OA0995D
All regions (NTSC)
BBC Opus Arte OABD7037D

La Fille mal gardée

Music: Hérold (arr. Lanchbery)
Choreography: Ashton
Cast: Nuñez, Acosta, Tuckett,
Howells
Orchestra of the Royal Opera
House/Twiner
Recorded 2005
BBC Opus Arte OA0992D
All regions (NTSC)
BBC Opus Arte OABD7021D

Giselle

Music: Adam (rev. Horovitz)
Choreography: Petipa
Cast: Cojocaru, Kobborg, Nuñez,
Harvey
Orchestra of the Royal Opera
House/Gruzin
Recorded 2006
DVD (BBC Opus Arte OA0993D)
All regions (NTSC)
Blu-ray (BBC Opus Arte
OABD7030D)

Sylvia

Music: Delibes
Choreography: Ashton
Cast: Bussell, Bolle, Soares, Harvey,
Galeazzi, Artists of The Royal Ballet
Orchestra of the Royal Opera
House/Bond
Recorded 2005
DVD (BBC Opus Arte OA0986D)
All regions (NTSC)
Blu-ray (BBC Opus Arte
OABD7030D)

The Firebird/Les Noces

Music: Stravinsky
Choreography: Fokine/Nijinska
Cast: Benjamin, Cope/Yanowsky,
Pickering
Orchestra of the Royal Opera
House/Carewe
Recorded 2001
Plus: film of Stravinsky conducting
The Firebird Suite
DVD (Opus Arte OA0832D)
All regions (NTSC)

Coppélia

Music: Delibes
Choreography: De Valois
Cast: Benjamin, Acosta, Heydon,
Artists of The Royal Ballet
Orchestra of the Royal Opera
House/Moldoveanu
Recorded 2000
All regions (NTSC)

www.roh.org.uk/rbshop

Books

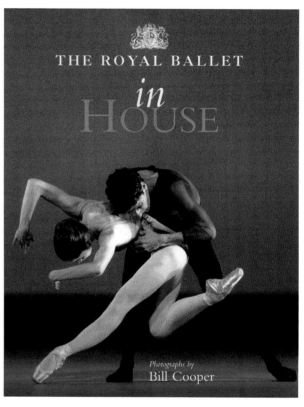

Pas de deux: The Royal Ballet in Pictures

Over 200 photographs of 53 ballets, in rehearsal and performance.
Oberon Books, 2007

ISBN 978-1-84002-777-8

In House

In House, photographs of The Royal Ballet by Bill Cooper, records the first three years of performances in the newly refurbished Royal Opera House. Over 200 photographs of 43 ballets are featured.

Oberon Books, 2002

ISBN 978-1-84002-350-3

Rudolph Nureyev and The Royal Ballet

Black and white photographs documenting Rudolph Nureyev's long association with The Royal Ballet, edited by Cristina Franchi.

Oberon Books, 2005

ISBN 978-1-84002-462-3

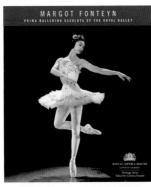

Margot Fonteyn: Prima Ballerina Assoluta of The Royal Ballet

Black and white photographs documenting Dame Margot Fonteyn's long association with The Royal Ballet, edited by Cristina Franchi.

Oberon Books, 2004

ISBN 978-1-84002-460-9

Frederick Ashton: Founder Choreographer of The Royal Ballet

Black and white photographs documenting Sir Frederick Ashton's career and ballets made for The Royal Ballet, edited by Cristina Franchi.

Oberon Books, 2004

ISBN 978-1-84002-461-6

Robert Helpmann; a Servant of Art

By Anna Bemrose

A comprehensive biography of Sir Robert Helpmann, detailing his life in dance, film and theatre.

UQP, 2009

ISBN 978-0-7022-3678-5

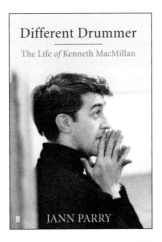

Different Drummer: the Life of Kenneth MacMillan

By Jann Parry

The first complete biography of Kenneth MacMillan.

Faber & Faber, 2009

ISBN 978-0-57124-302-0

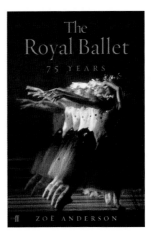

The Royal Ballet: 75 years

By Zoë Anderson

A history of The Royal Ballet since its inception to the present day.

Faber & Faber, 2006

ISBN 978-0-57122-795-2

Freddy

OFFICIAL SPONSOR AND SUPPLIER OF DANCE AND SPORT FASHION WEAR TO THE ROYAL BALLET

For the 2010/11 Season Italian dance and sport fashion wear company Freddy continues its partnership with The Royal Ballet as official sponsor and supplier of dance and sport fashion wear for the Company.

Together they created the Freddy Royal Ballet Dancers' Collection, unique to the dancers, and a Freddy Royal Ballet collection available in Freddy stores worldwide, the Royal Opera House Shop, and online. The collection includes jackets, leggings, towels, a range of bags and accessories, and exclusive souvenir t-shirts.

Visit www.freddy.it or come into the Royal Opera House shop.

Royal Ballet Principal Federico Bonelli models some of the exclusive Freddy Royal Ballet Dancers' Collection.

FREDDY